I0714440

Second Site

POINT
____

SERIES EDITOR   Sarah Whiting

Second Site, James Nisbet
Lateness, Peter Eisenman with Elisa Iturbe
After Art, David Joselit
Kissing Architecture, Sylvia Lavin

Second Site

James Nisbet

Princeton University Press   Princeton and Oxford

Published by Princeton University Press, 41 William Street, Princeton, New Jersey 08540

In the United Kingdom: Princeton University Press, 6 Oxford Street, Woodstock, Oxfordshire OX20 1TR

press.princeton.edu

Library of Congress Cataloging-in-Publication Data
Names: Nisbet, James, 1981- author.
Title: Second site / James Nisbet.

Description: Princeton : Princeton University Press, [2021] | Series: Point: essays on architecture | Includes bibliographical references.

Identifiers: LCCN 2021018390 (print) | LCCN 2021018391 (ebook) | ISBN 9780691194950 (paperback) | ISBN 9780691224961 (ebook)

Subjects: LCSH: Earthworks (Art) | Earthworks (Art)—Conservation and restoration. | Time and art. | BISAC: ART / Environmental & Land Art | ART / History / Contemporary (1945-)

Classification: LCC N6494.E27 N57 2021 (print) | LCC N6494.E27 (ebook) | DDC 709.04/076—dc23

LC record available at https://lccn.loc.gov/2021018390

LC ebook record available at https://lccn.loc.gov/2021018391
British Library Cataloging-in-Publication Data is available

This book has been composed in Helvetica Neue and Scala
Printed on acid-free paper. ∞
Printed in China
10 9 8 7 6 5 4 3 2 1

For my family

Contents

Series Editor's Preface

POINT offers a new cadence to contemporary conversations about design. Deliberately situated between the pithy polemic and the heavily footnoted tome, POINT plumbs the world of the extended essay. Each essay in this series hones a single point while situating it within a broader discursive landscape, thereby simultaneously focusing and fueling aesthetic criticism. The agility of POINT's format permits leading theorists, historians, and practitioners to take the pulse of the field for an informed, interested public.

At the center of James Nisbet's provocative essay *Second Site* lies a truism that, while seemingly simple, ultimately yanks the ground from underneath us: *sites are not stable*. Instead, they are actors within an entire ecology, or even ecologies, connecting social, cultural, aesthetic, economic, and political histories, geological evolutions, property changes, natural disasters, and human-centered caprices—layers upon layers that complete, extend, or entirely contradict site-specific artworks and monuments.

Nisbet's intellectually generous essay cultivates close attention while never restricting its frame, addressing with fluidity and sensitivity issues ranging from indigenous land rights to authorial intention and material fabrication. Nisbet promises a second site; at the end of the day, he delivers so many more.

—*Sarah Whiting*

Acknowledgments

My sincere thanks to the many people and institutions who made the research and site visits for this book possible, including Lisa Le Feuvre, Wilhelmine Hellmann, Hanna Johansson, Peter Krieger, P. J. Brownlee, and Jon Revett. I am also indebted to conversations with Amanda Boetzkes, Mark Cheetham, T. J. Demos, Francesca Esmay, Daniel Hackbarth, Elizabeth Hutchinson, Caroline Jones, Aaron Katzeman, Louie Provost, Rebecca Urchill, and Edward Vazquez, whose insights were immeasurably helpful in shaping the argument. Many artists were generous in sharing and discussing their work; I am grateful to Bonnie Devine, Simone Estrin, Edgar Heap of Birds, Chip Lord, Richard Serra, Alan Sonfist, and Trina McKeever at the Richard Serra Studio. An invitation from the Clark Art Institute (Christopher P. Heuer, Rebecca Zorach, and Michael Ann Holly) was formative to this project, and support from the Getty Research Institute and the Humanities Center at UC Irvine were invaluable for bringing it to completion. My thanks to all of the "Art and Ecology" fellows at the GRI for a year of inspiring dialogue, and to the students at UC Irvine, who made a memorable trek with me to visit several of the sites discussed in this book. It has been a true pleasure to work with Princeton University Press, and I'm thankful to Michelle Komie for her unflagging support of this project, the anonymous peer reviewers for their most valuable notes, and Sarah Whiting for her thoughtful responses throughout the entire process. The majority of this book was written in Los Angeles and Irvine, California, and I wish to acknowledge my presence as a settler art historian on the traditional, ancestral, and unceded homelands of the Gabrielino/Tongva and Acjachemen peoples. This text has taken shape over years of sojourns near and far, many shared and inspired by my parents, Anne and Jay. During those years, I had the supreme pleasure of welcoming Julia and Josie into the world. This book is dedicated to these cherished members of my family, and especially to Jessica, whose opinion I always seek out first and whose brilliant company I'll revere to the last.

Preface

What does it mean to say that we are on a site? To be at a *location*, in *position*, to have found the *spot*—all seem to strike at something similar, but don't quite hit the mark. For a site is a patch of earth that not only warrants our attention, for one reason or another, but also brings further expectation that something is going to happen there, or maybe already has. Location, spot, environment, area, and so on—these all describe the space itself. A site, however, intimates more. Similar to a *place* and the liveliness of place-making, a site is a space that has been worked, whether that work be actual labor or the conception of a design, singular activity or myriad enterprises, conscious plans or unforeseen episodes. *This is the site of* . . . . It is the inkling of these further activities that turns a location into a site.

But just as sites can come to be entangled with the things that happen in their environs, so too can things come to belong to their sites. That the Egyptian pyramids belong to a stretch of a few hundred miles along the Nile River, or Europe's premodern cathedrals occupy a smattering of specific plots across the continent, seems self-evident. But when other similarly grand edifices end up elsewhere—London Bridge, for instance, being shipped in pieces and reassembled at Lake Havasu in Arizona—it raises the question of whether the commitment to a site is intrinsic to large-scale constructions or is more an assumption based on the practical difficulty of relocating them (figure 1). London Bridge's transatlantic move was prompted by a combination of human and environmental considerations. A "modern" stone bridge had been erected in the 1830s to replace a crumbling medieval structure that did not accommodate London's growing boat traffic on the Thames River. But the design of this new bridge, in turn, could not have anticipated the arrival of the mass and volume of automobiles a century later, causing it to sink into the ground at an unsustainable rate.[1] In need of a bridge and also a marketing device to promote the new planned desert community of Lake Havasu City, an American entrepreneur purchased the entire edifice for $2.4 million. This story of London Bridge is instructive about the ways in which structures take on new demands and cultural connotations over time, but it also underscores the fact that such structures are only pragmatically bound to their original sites rather than being bound to them as a requirement of their existence.

Since the 1960s, however, a group of artworks have emerged that are more deliberately intended to exist in

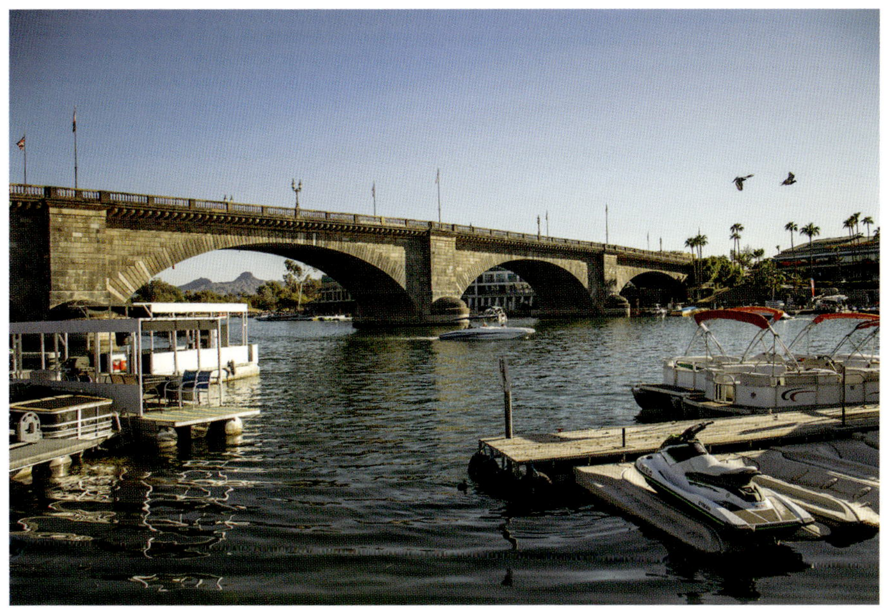

only one place. Termed "site-specific art," this body of work is most closely associated with land art, a movement forged during the '60s among artists who began to incorporate organic materials and outdoor environments directly into the production of their work.[2] Sometimes called earth art or earthworks, land art describes a number of such practices that arose internationally and largely independently of one another, but which became increasingly legible as a shared tendency through group exhibitions staged in the United States and Europe.[3] Not all land art is site-specific, but

Figure 1. John Rennie, London Bridge, 1799–1831/1971, Lake Havasu, Arizona; photograph: Tara Watkins, 2020

its most celebrated works were indeed created outdoors, the prime examples of which have become significant tourist attractions in their own right. Robert Smithson's *Spiral Jetty* (1970) is a 1,500-foot coil of rocks and dirt in the Great Salt Lake. As of 2017, it is now the official artwork of the state of Utah. Michael Heizer's *Double Negative* (1969) was shaped by excavating two huge trenches on the Mormon Mesa in Nevada that face one another to form a massive prism of negative space across the expanse. Nancy Holt's *Sun Tunnels* (1973–1976) consists of four large concrete cylinders set into the Great Basin Desert in Utah and configured in an "X" that aligns with the setting sun of the summer and winter solstices (figure 2). Walter De Maria's *Lightning Field* (1977) in New Mexico, a grid of four hundred stainless steel rods, does indeed catch the occasional bolt of lightning in late summer, but each and every day throughout the year it also plays with reflections of sunlight cast across the celestial vault of the high desert.

Yet when we think of the spaces in which the monuments of land art were sited, and especially the photographs of them that circulate in books and online, these sites seem to dwell in the past, in stilled images of deserts, lakes, and mesas now some fifty years old. Many are pictures of the American West that reverberate with the mythos of that region's desert expanses as lifeless and timeless landscapes. From the trails crossing the West that were traveled by the small cadre in

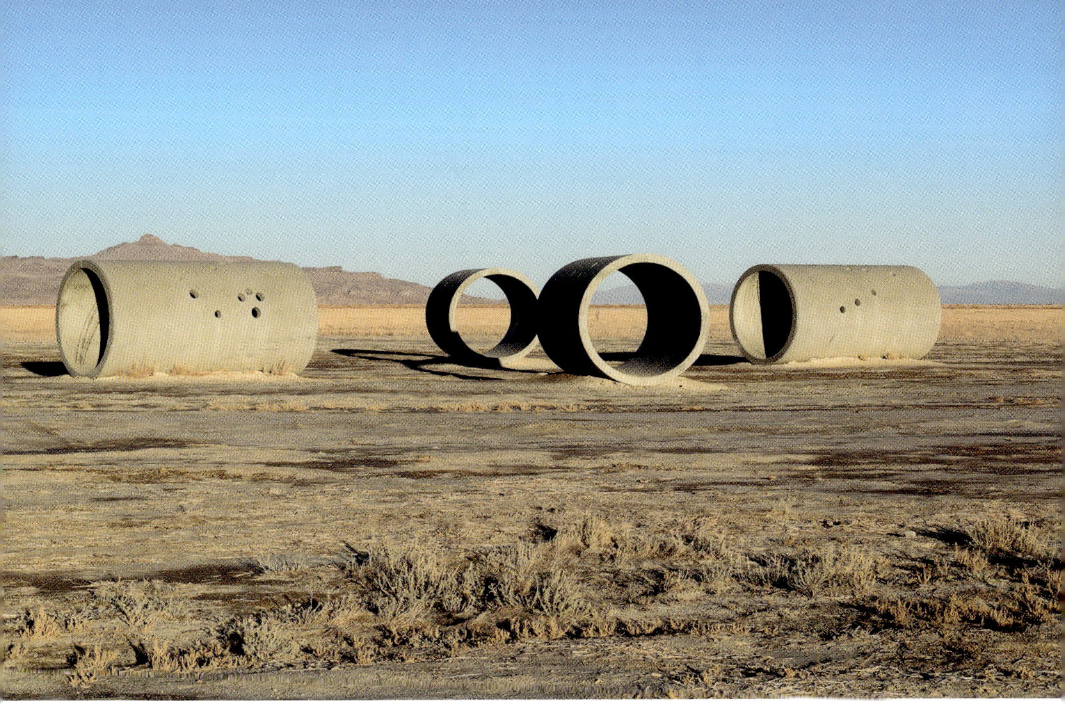

John Ford's *Stagecoach* (1939) to the West Texas plains pictured in the sweeping pans of the Coen brothers' *No Country for Old Men* (2007), the Western terrain has consistently been etched in our cultural imaginary as a passive setting.[4] But just like the West itself, the sites of land art have never been static. At *Spiral Jetty*, Smithson had anticipated the fluctuating level of the Great Salt Lake as part of his piece's site-specificity, but before his untimely death in 1973 he certainly could not have foreseen the climatological alterations and severe droughts in Utah that now consistently keep the water's edge hundreds of yards from his earthwork (figure 3).

Figure 2. Nancy Holt, Sun Tunnels, 1973–1976, Great Basin Desert, Utah; photograph: James Nisbet, 2018

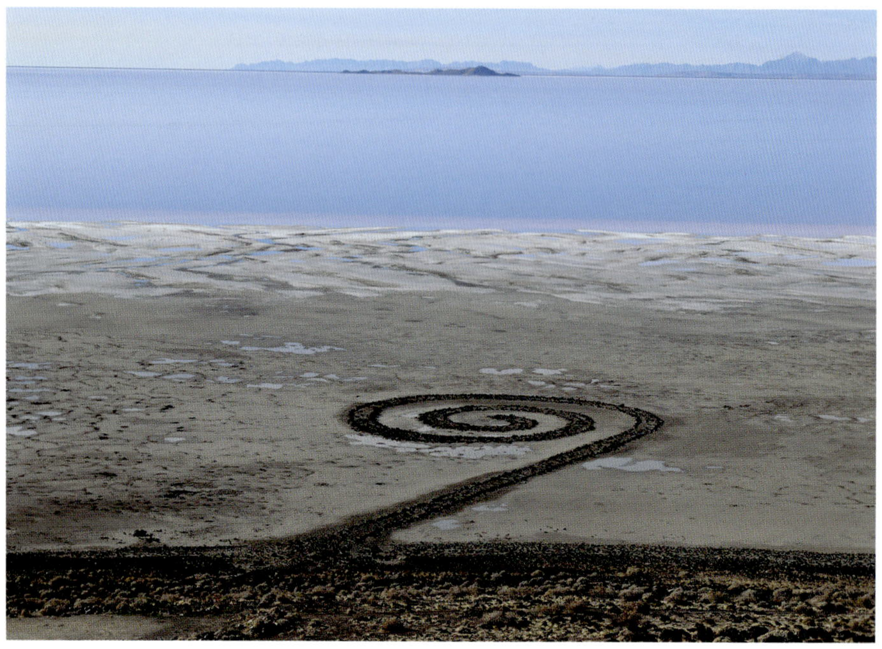

The work's present condition is perhaps all the more significant if we consider that *Spiral Jetty* was created during a low ebb in the lake's water level, and that, soon after completion, Smithson's piece spent the next three decades completely submerged. That *Spiral Jetty* is now rarely covered in water of any depth shows just how dramatic the local changes to this site have been since the 1970s. Yet while the vicissitudes of *Spiral Jetty* have been well documented, equally significant alterations to other site-specific artworks have not.

I have spent well over a decade visiting land art sites and have been consistently surprised and sometimes shocked to encounter their current conditions. Art historians typically gloss over such environmental changes by deeming an artwork to be falling into ruin or even disappearing. But if site-specific art is premised on the interrelation between work and site, then any changes to a site must also be understood to reverberate *with* the work that exists there, rather than simply diminishing it. What is required is a more ecological approach to understanding site-specificity. Ecology and its prefix kindred (ecocide, ecotourism, ecopolitics, ecocriticism) are often aligned quite strictly with caring for the environment, but in its more capacious sense ecology addresses the inherent reliance of things upon one another in order to exist. Ecological perspectives now increasingly guide interpretations of artworks and cultural activity more generally, addressing not only art that deals with "nature" but also intersections that encompass environmental justice, nonhuman animals, material cultures, and climate.[5] There has been scant attention, however, in this ecological turn of thought to the centrality of duration as a primary concern, though duration is the very means by which ecosystems are sustained. This is to say that it does not suffice to pay attention to ecological connectivity only as a slice in time. We must also attend to how such connections come in and out of being. By addressing the effects of longer stretches of time on sites and the structures they support, this book grapples with the continuities and discontinuities that accrue in the ecological *longue durée* of location.[6]

Second Site thus reflects less on site-specificity in and of itself, and more on new ways of thinking about how it twists and turns over time. I call the effects of these fluctuations "second sites" for several reasons. The first and most direct sense of meaning calls attention to the fact that no site is ever unchanging over the long run of time. Ever since Lessing's *Laocoon* (1766), ideas about time have been crucial to the experience of art within modernity, but the vast literature on temporality in the history of art tends to focus on time as a strictly cultural phenomenon.[7] The approach to ecology and time that I am proposing does not separate culture from nature, or vice versa, but instead maintains that each has a duration intermingled with the other's that cannot be isolated. For every initial site, second, third, and fourth ones will inevitably form, and on and on, from ceaseless and continuous ecological activity. The scientific name for this process is "succession" (to which we return momentarily).

In addition, "second site" also evokes the notion of "second nature." By this latter term, I don't mean a person's habits or intuitive responses. I refer instead to the idea that we as humans do not have access to a raw version of nature out in the world, or what might be called a "first nature." What we access has instead already been filtered through social constructs.[8] The implications of this insight for site-specificity are twofold: not only does a site transform from its "original" condition moving forward in time, but such a condition has already adapted from past states. Even at the moment at which an artwork is created, it already exists on a second site.

Finally, "second site" also plays upon the pseudoscientific belief in a "second sight" that allows its seer to sense things and events not immediately present before the eyes. Typically, second sight is associated with perceptions of phenomena that either are transpiring in distant places or will do so in the future. But when thinking about the changeability of artworks located outdoors, second sight also invokes the moments and states of an artwork from its past that have since been altered and can no longer be tangibly experienced. These prior states of a site do not cease to matter once they pass. Instead, they continue to matter through a kind of awareness that is no longer directly present to someone on-site, being accessible only in media such as photography, verbal records, and other forms of memorialization. As inherently ecological, the secondness of sites is sustained by the interdependence of all of these elements, which depend on one another in synchrony but also exist along their own time lines.

The picture that I have in mind of this condition finds a useful analogue in an experimental film called

Zorns Lemma (1970), which was made by the artist and polymath Hollis Frampton (figure 4). Like many of the figures of interest to *Second Site*, Frampton was deeply influenced by the natural sciences, as reflected in films such as *Maxwell's Demon* (1968), which is named for a nineteenth-century thought experiment in thermodynamics created by James Clerk Maxwell.[9] In similar fashion, *Zorns Lemma* derives its title from a mathematical proposition in set theory named after the German-born American mathematician Max Zorn.[10] Frampton's film also creates a kind of set: twenty-four letters of the alphabet, cycling onscreen at one-second intervals from shots taken on the streets of Manhattan. The cycle begins with someone holding the letter "A" from a sign, then the handwritten word "baby," then "CABINET" written on a glass window, and so on through the entire alphabet minus the letters I/J and U. Frampton truncated these letters to reach the key number of twenty-four, matching the speed of twenty-four frames per second required during projection to achieve the illusion that the sixteen-millimeter still frames of *Zorns Lemma* are in motion. As the film progresses, repeatedly cycling from A to Z, certain letters begin to be substituted with shots of other actions—"K" for a man painting a wall, "N" for a container being filled with beans, "E" for a person walking on the street. Some of these actions, like painting a wall and filling a container, lead to a conclusion, while others, such as

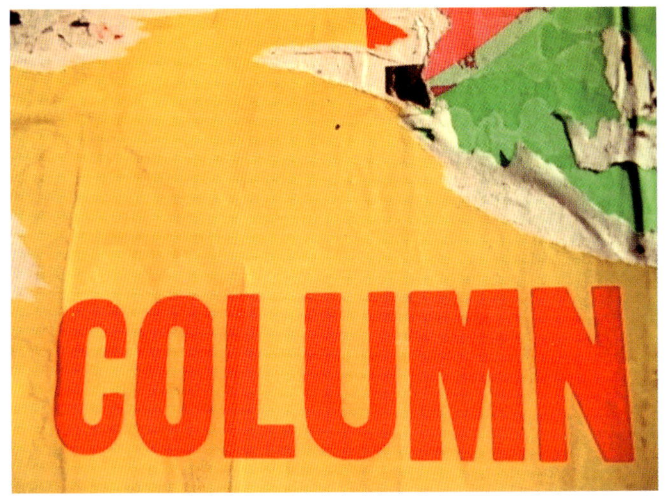

Figure 4. Hollis Frampton, Zorns Lemma, film still, 1970

steam pouring out of a pipe ("Q") and waves breaking against a shore ("Z"), are more indefinite in duration. Watching this film, I would like to suggest, offers a rich meditation for thinking about site. All of the parts assembled contribute to creating the whole, but each also unfolds in time on its own terms. *One or many environments?* While *Zorns Lemma* offers an evocative approach to picturing a response to this question, its limitations for doing so stem from the fact that environments don't follow predictable rules. Nor do they reach finite conclusions.

Thus, it is critical to distinguish the unpredictable and structural kind of ecological change described by the notion of second site from other types of environmental alterations that are more foreseeable and minimal in nature. A prime example of the latter is weathering. As Mohsen Mostafavi and David Leatherbarrow poignantly write, "weathering . . . exchanges the roles of art and nature. In design, art is assumed to be the power or agency that *forms* nature; in the life or time of a construction, however, nature *re-forms* the 'finished' art work."[11] In the transformation they describe, a veneer ages, taking on a patina that registers that passing of time. In this understanding of weathering, there is a playful inversion of what it means to finish a project. Under the agency of the designer, "finish" is the perfecting of planned surfaces, whereas under the agency of weather, surface becomes an interface between that design and the more haphazard actions of nature. But while Mostafavi and Leatherbarrow maintain that weathering ultimately "re-forms" a work, I would push against this claim to instead parse the difference between surface and structure. Weathering changes facade and appearance, while secondness alters more fundamental relationships to site.

To draw out this thought a little further, we might consider two sites near one another in the Tampere region in southwestern Finland. Through the advocacy of a local arts collective, gravel quarries in the region were offered to Nancy Holt and to the Hungarian-born artist Agnes Denes to create new earthworks that would reclaim these ravaged sites as aesthetic spaces.

Holt's contribution, *Up and Under* (1998), builds upon the same visual language as her earlier *Sun Tunnels,* using concrete tunnels to create passageways of movement that also frame and syncopate the visual field of the environment that visitors experience as they walk around the site.[12] Built into the shape of a meandering serpent—in dialogue with ancient earthworks in Western Europe and Indigenous ones in the Americas—*Up and Under* was originally designed to include a path across the top of the structure and three circular pools of water around its base. The current condition of the work approximates this original arrangement, but with notable differences (figures 5 and 6). The cement has aged, revealing chips and cracking—so much so in the base of the pools that their water has long departed. There is still a path along the top of the mound, but now several unplanned and less formal paths have appeared, created by visitors walking up and down its vertical slope. In addition, mining was maintained in the quarry up until the year 2003, an activity that piled waste in the vicinity of Holt's landforms and damaged the irrigation system.[13] Although all these changes have left their mark on *Up and Under*—to a stunning degree, judging from photographs taken as recently as the late 1990s—the essential experience of the work remains the same. Though minor restoration has been carried out since that time to clear the ground of debris and invasive plant growth, *Up and Under* still works

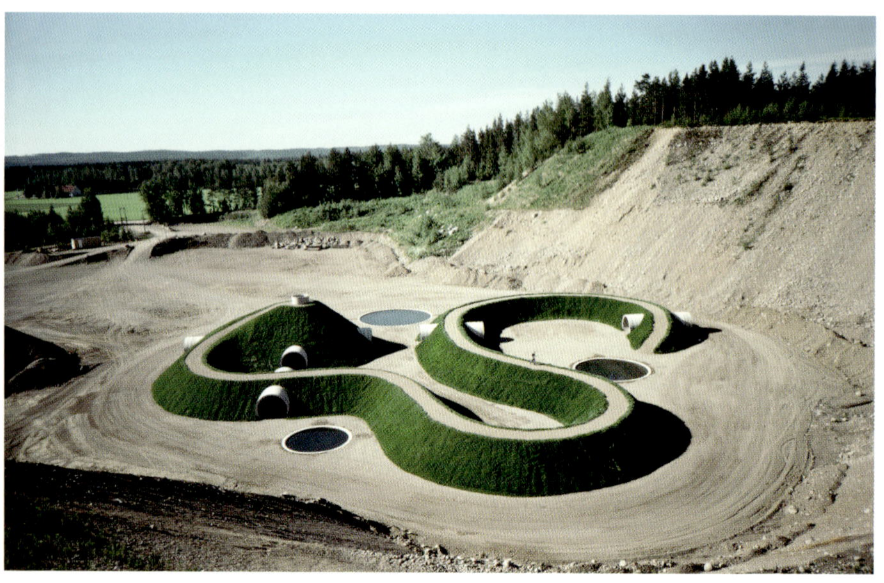

predominantly through its modulation of spatial movement and viewpoint, even as the site continues to slowly transition from quarry back to forest. In the long run of time, *Up and Under* may cease to be recognizable as the same artwork, but today that more substantial alteration has yet to happen. Akin to the heavily eroded chasms that visitors now encounter at Heizer's *Double Negative*, the shell of *Up and Under* has noticeably *weathered*, yet the primary experience of the work remains essentially unaltered.

The relative continuity in the aesthetic experience of *Up and Under* differs markedly from that of Denes's *Tree*

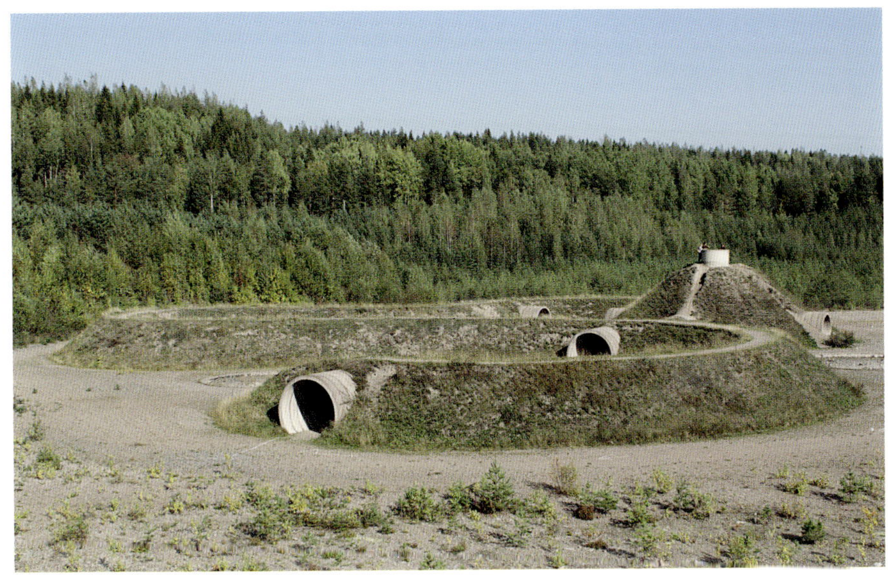

Mountain. Located a short distance away, *Tree Mountain* has been more profoundly affected by the passing of time (figures 7 and 8). It was originally conceived by Denes in 1982 as a "living time capsule" of trees planted according to an intricate geometrical spiral; her vision came to fruition a decade later, when the government of Finland announced at the 1992 Earth Summit in Rio de Janeiro that it would sponsor her piece. Denes initially planned a forest of ten thousand trees to be individually planted by ten thousand people, with each person holding the right of ownership to their tree for a period of four hundred years. In the artist's words,

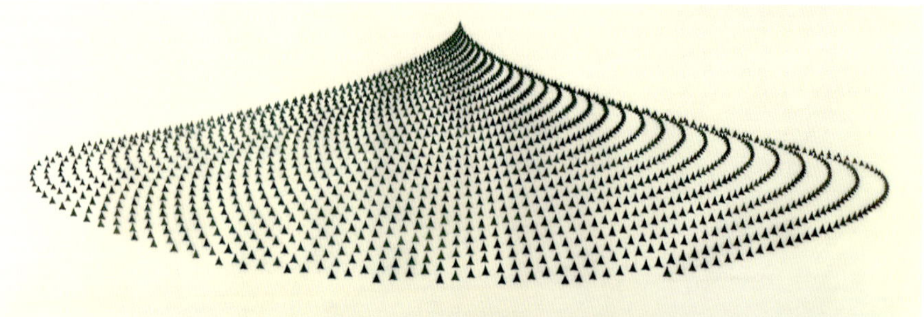

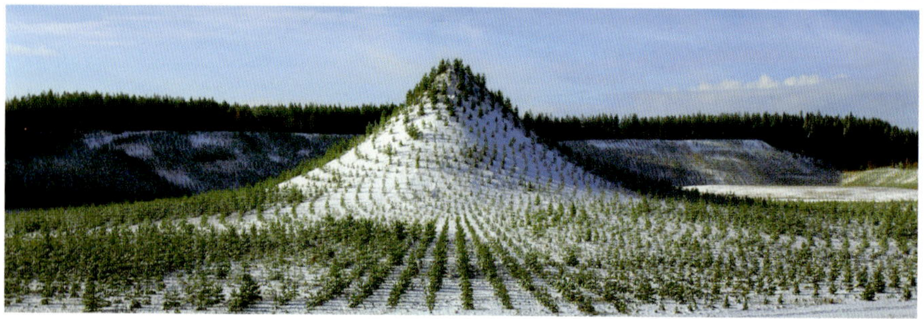

Though they may be salable, collective and inheritable commodities—gaining stature, fame and value as they grow and age as trees—ultimately neither can be truly owned. One can only become a custodian and assume the moral obligations it implies. In the meanwhile the trees remain part of a larger whole, the forest. Individual segments of a single, limited edition, the trees are unique patterns in the design of their own universe. And the trees live on through the centuries—stable and majestic, outliving their owners and custodians who created the patterns and the philosophy but not the tree.[14]

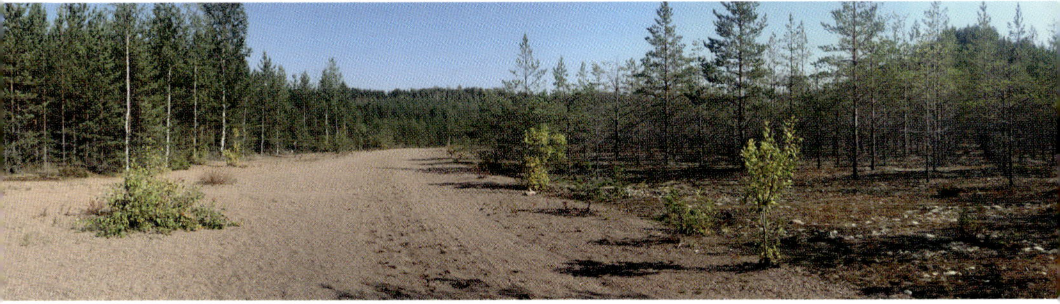

Denes paints a beautiful mental image here: a curving array of old-growth forest quietly abiding in its own universe amid the chaos of the world beyond its confines. But in reality, no environment can be so encapsulated, in time or otherwise. Now in its third decade, *Tree Mountain* was in fact planted with some eleven thousand trees by eleven thousand participants, exceeding Denes's original expectation. Not all of these trees, however, are currently on course to reach the "majestic" stature envisioned by the artist. Amid a monoculture of conifers planted in soil that had been severely degraded by the former mining operation there, many of the trees in Denes's work have either died or been drastically stunted. Walking the gravel of the mile-long road that forms an elliptical ring around the work gives the walker a striking view of just how diminished the grounds of *Tree Mountain* appear in comparison to the density and diversity of the uncultivated forest

Figure 8. Agnes Denes, Tree Mountain—A Living Time Capsule—11,000 Trees, 11,000 People, 400 Years, 420 × 270 × 28 meters, Ylöjärvi, Finland, 1992–1996; photograph: Jessica Johnston, 2019

to the other side. In short, the passing of time at *Tree Mountain* has seen changes to the site that move beyond the pale of "weathering." What this work now communicates about monocultural agronomy and the effects of soil degradation exceeds its original intentions and planned design.

Rather than a merely weathered earthwork, I would designate *Tree Mountain* a second site, one whose ecological fluctuations and adaptations have proven more influential over time than was anticipated at its moment of creation. Cast more broadly, the implications for this kind of ecological duration are immense. We are accustomed to attributing the meaning of cultural objects to their maker, but what happens when the lives of such objects spiral into the orbit of other, often anonymous, and sometimes nonhuman creators and contributors? We likewise tend to think of the history of art and architectural objects as being intimately tied to the time of their making, but what if new versions of the same work arise that obliterate the very possibility of experiencing that earlier "original"? In 1964, the art critic and philosopher Arthur Danto coined the term "artworld" to describe a system through which innovative artworks expand our understanding of what art is and can be. The arrival of something innovative on the scene—Danto's primary example being a then-recent exhibition of Andy Warhol's *Brillo Boxes,* which are silkscreened replicas of the actual packing containers for Brillo scrub pads—prompts us to enfold new categories into our imagination of what constitutes the world of art. Or, in Danto's evocative language, "The artworld stands to the real world in something like the relationship in which the City of God stands to the Earthly City."[15] Following Danto's terms, the land art that began to appear but a few years later might be understood as an attempted bridge between advanced sculptural ideas drawn from that City of God (the art world) and actual outdoor sites of the Earthly City (the real world). But as critics such as the anthropologist Alfred Gell have noted, the gates of Danto's particular "artworld" were open only to new additions that fit the conventions of authorship and intention in the Western tradition of art.[16] Second sites are not so orthodox.

I have introduced second sites, or what I would more generally call a condition of "secondness," as a notion for working through what visitors now encounter at places such as *Spiral Jetty* or *Tree Mountain*.[17] But secondness itself is not a singular or reductive concept. There are such diverse and unpredictable means by which sites can be altered and speeds at which that can occur. At the time of writing these words in the summer of 2020, for instance, a one-acre fire in San Francisco's Presidio national park has charred Andy Goldsworthy's *Spire,* a one-hundred-foot-tall, site-specific sculpture installed in 2008 with the trunks of thirty-seven Monterey cypress trees cut down as part of a reforestation

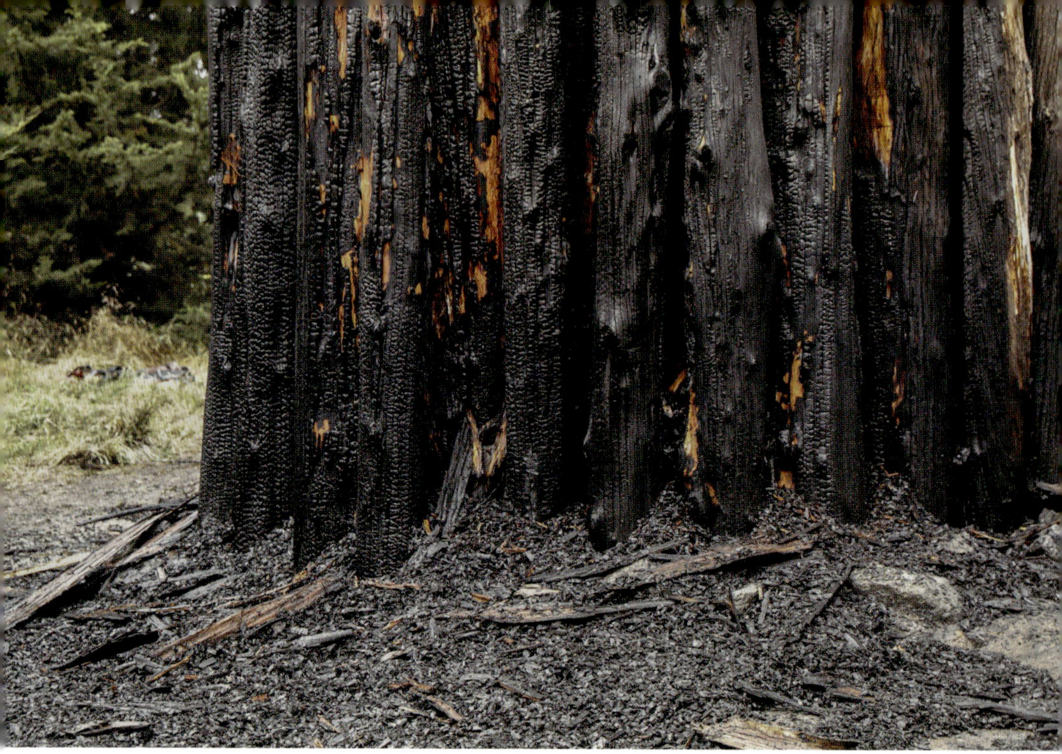

plan in the park (figure 9). *Spire* was made to be eventually absorbed by the forest around it and, as such, to be a symbol of and marker for the slow time of regenerative growth and decay in forests. Yet from a fire that lasted but a matter of hours, its damaged exterior now registers a more explosive experience of time, its cracked and blackened surface evoking the increasingly devastating wildfires that appear annually in places as distant as Australia and as nearby as *Spire*'s home state of California.[18] Whether applied to the type of abrupt change that struck *Spire* or the longer-term environmental conditions affecting land art sites, secondness is a term for grappling with the volatility that attends ecological duration.

To call secondness a condition of ecology, however, does not mean that its effects are produced by biology or climate alone. Ecology instead embraces these "natural" processes as much as it does the social history of places and the generations of transformation that have occurred in them.[19] With respect to the North American continent in particular, scholars of Indigenous histories and environmental rights make clear that any encounter with "wilderness"—whether in the protected lands of national parks or otherwise—is already marked by centuries of colonial occupation and violent seizure.[20] Purely personal or phenomenological encounters with such environments are a fantasy of firstness that turns a blind eye to the weight and severity of that history. Indeed, the fundamental challenge of attending to the temporalities that sustain any site over time is recognizing the sheer diversity of the biological and social activities that have converged there in the past and continue to do so in the present. This is an especially urgent task during a political period in which claims about the naturalness or inherent possession of territories are increasingly summoned to discriminate against the equal right of all to live and to work, as well as a climatological task as we witness increasingly unbridled catastrophe. While the ideas articulated in this book have grown out of my personal experience of visiting the sites discussed, its central claim is not about these particular experiences, or even about site-specific art per se. This body of artwork instead offers an especially apt vehicle through which to foster an attentiveness to sites that bears not only on visual art and aesthetics but also on the ethics of how we understand and treat the vast array of different places on our planet. *Second Site* is a primer for cultivating such a practice of attention and recognition.

Second Site

Succession

Turning to the science of ecology, one of the additional difficulties posed by addressing site-specific artworks arises from a friction between the actuality of their ecological condition and our terminology for understanding it. In other words, it is inevitable that living environments will adapt, but our concepts for explaining that adaptation are shaped by the specific methods of their corresponding academic disciplines. Artworks might compel us to draw from ideas in the natural sciences, but those ideas themselves must morph in order to make sense with respect to art. What results are layers of what ecology might mean to specific fields. There is a technical field of ecology sustained by scientific specialists, an ecology that attends to cultural objects, and an ecological interrelation that joins these various systems of thought and practice together.

The artwork *Shift* by the American sculptor Richard Serra is an uncommonly pertinent example for thinking through this kind of cross-communication between art and science (figures 10 and 11). Consisting of a series of low-lying walls situated on farmland in King City, Ontario—a small community located just north of Toronto—*Shift* has experienced a remarkable range of alterations since its creation in the early 1970s. The walls were placed by Serra and the artist Joan Jonas following their prolonged exercise of moving through and inhabiting the land. By Serra's telling of it,

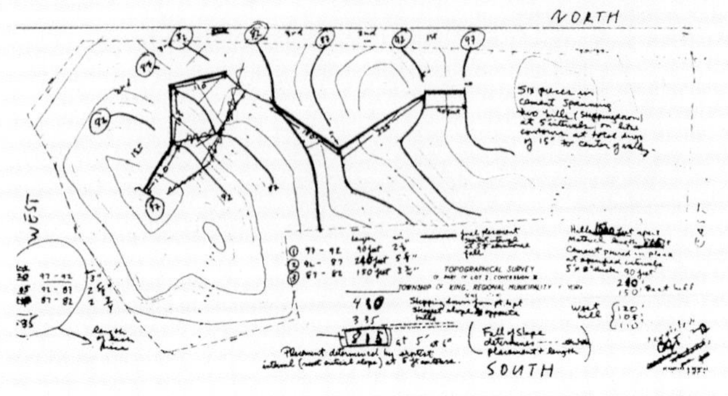

In the summer of 1970, Joan and I spent five days walking the place. We discovered that two people walking the distance of the field opposite one another, attempting to keep each other in view despite the curvature of the land, would mutually determine a topological definition of the space. The boundaries of the work became the maximum distance two people could occupy and still keep each other in view. . . . What I wanted was a dialectic between one's perception of the place in totality and one's relation to the field as walked. The result is a way of measuring oneself against the indeterminacy of the land.[1]

This intertwined relationship between movement, visibility, and topography would inform *Shift*'s final composition: six slabs of poured concrete, eight inches wide, each guided in direction and length by the contours of the site, which Serra resurveyed in the planning stages at a grade of one-foot intervals.[2] Beginning at the two extreme points of distance set out by his and Jonas's

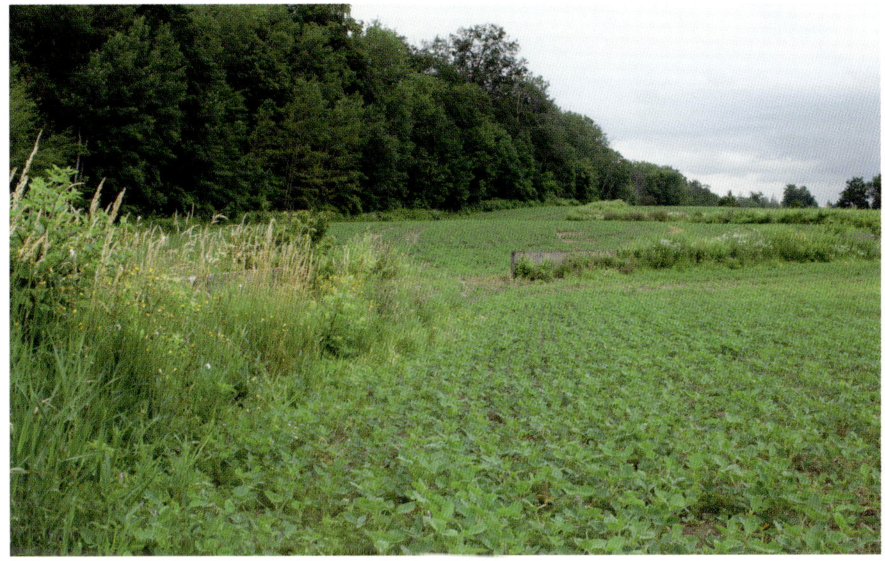

movement through the field, Serra erected walls in the direction of the most significant drop in elevation, extending each wall until this vertical drop reached a height of five feet. Varying in length and direction, the three walls on each side of the field zig and zag toward the three walls on the other, meeting in an open space in the center.

When Serra refers to "the place" in which *Shift* is located, he seems most interested in its shape; he essentially treats place as a combination of topography and space. But the place in which *Shift* exists might be understood to also encompass its community and

Figure 11. Richard Serra, *Shift*, 1970–1972, King City, Ontario, concrete, six sections: 60" × 90' × 8"; 60" × 240' × 8"; 60" × 150' × 8"; 60" × 120' × 8"; 60" × 110' × 8"; 60" × 105' × 8"; photograph: James Nisbet, 2017

the species that live in and around the field in which the work is located. These aspects of *Shift*'s site have changed quite distinctly since 1972, a transformation all the more pointed considering that the sculpture and its parcel of land are owned by the Toronto-based development company Hickory Hill Investments, having been purchased from Serra's original patron, Roger Davidson, when he sold his farmland in 1974.[3] Hickory Hill then ignored the presence of *Shift* on the land it bought for thirty years, until 2004, when members of King Township's city council moved to register the artwork as a heritage site. During approximately the same period of time, Hickory Hill had begun to build condominiums and single-family homes on its real estate holdings in King City. In the span of a few short years, this development significantly altered the demographics and organization of the town: a small rural, agricultural community became a growing exurb of nearby Toronto. Though these rapid alterations to King City generated uncertainty about the future of *Shift*, Hickory Hill staunchly resisted attempts to legally protect Serra's sculpture and site, claiming that any such designation was "inappropriate and unnecessary" for what the company described as "a private piece of art on private property" that was already protected by an environmental preservation act named after the local Oak Ridges Moraine.[4] This legislation had been passed in 2001 to control growth within the lands immediately north of Toronto, protecting its wildlife and water quality. To claim it as protection for an artwork, however, is a more complicated matter, as the Oak Ridges Moraine Conservation Act limits construction but doesn't strictly prohibit it.[5] It wouldn't, for instance, prevent condominiums from being constructed around the work, or its field from being turned into a city park. To claim that such measures inherently protect site-specific artworks confuses environmental conservation with cultural heritage conservation. We turn to art preservation in more detail later, but to state the difference succinctly here, environmental conservation strives to protect "ecological and hydrological integrity," in the language of the Oak Ridges Moraine Act, while cultural heritage conservation is concerned with protecting artistic intent. In other words, one acts to maintain ongoing relationships in an environment, while the other focuses on the integrity of how an artwork is experienced by its spectator.

The suburbanization of King City is only part of the story of *Shift*. The annual cycles of the agricultural seasons and the accelerating changes to global climate have also had an impact on the work. We might consider, for instance, what it is like to see *Shift* during the late summer and early fall in a year when its field is planted with corn and its sculptural walls must be sought out through blind exploration amid the tall stalks growing across the site. Even when the walls have been located, the restricted visibility of the cornfield limits the view to no more than one or two walls at any one time. In such conditions, the walls are not markers rising up from the flat topography of the land, as Serra described them, but rather pathways, sunken beneath the tops of the stalks, through the dense, all-over vegetation. Even when planted with a lower-lying crop, like soybeans, *Shift* can be significantly affected by local weather. During years with intense rains in the spring, wild plants grow up around the sides of the work that almost entirely cover its walls, leaving them visible only in small patches. In this state, the shape of the land might well be visible, but the shape of the sculpture becomes something left more to the imagination. Across such extreme experiences of seeing the field covered by full stalks of corn or the walls engulfed by overgrowth, the relationship between sculptural object and environment remains vital to *Shift* and its site. The work is still site-specific, just not according to the formal lines and planes of the sculpture Serra conceived in the early 1970s. Instead of being strictly a visible shape, the sculptural presence of *Shift* has taken on more dynamic relationships with the living aspects of its environment.

The kind of change that *Shift* has undergone is difficult to describe with the language currently available to discussions of art and architecture. By way of counterexample, the variations to both the immediate site and the larger civic footprint of *Shift* are more systemic

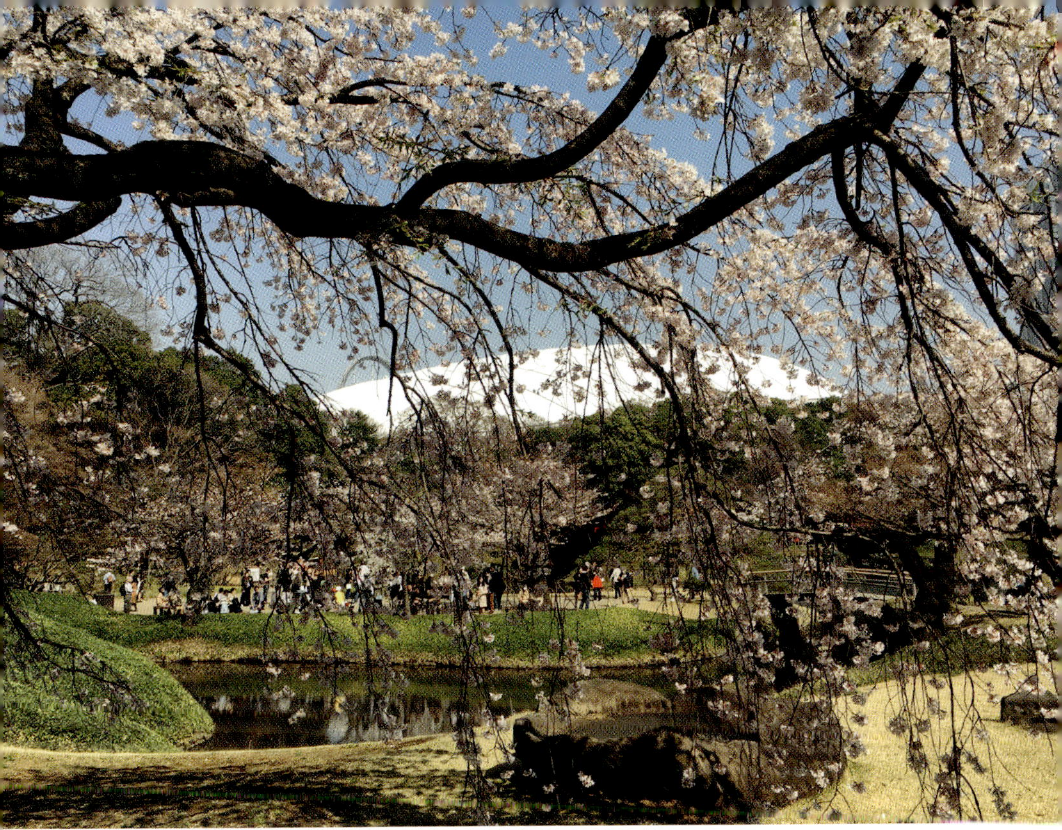

than most encroachments of urban development on the fringes of other sites. In Tokyo, for instance, the white, air-supported roof atop the 1980s-era Tokyo Dome now hovering above the city's historic Koishikawa Korakuen Garden has undoubtedly changed that garden's sight lines, but it hasn't fundamentally changed the garden itself (figure 12). Designed in the seventeenth century to incorporate a combination of recognizable landscapes from both Japan and China, Korakuen is a place that

Figure 12. Mito Yorifusa and Mito Mitsukuni, Koishikawa Korakuen Garden, seventeenth century, Tokyo, Japan; photograph: 2018

invites reflection on the passing of time in temporalities that range from the mere days of a flower's bloom to the years and even millennia that have shaped the rocks populating sections of the garden. In contrast, the Tokyo Dome's disruptive, techno-industrial presence looms large. It, too, invites reflection on the passing of time, but not through internal rumination so much as by evincing more external and unwieldy growth. Rather than adding to the biological and geological cycles of time cultivated within the garden, its presence is closer to montage—a collision of two images, each of a different temporal order and origin. Unlike the gradual and more thorough transformation of *Shift* and its site, the intrusion of the Tokyo Dome on Korakuen presents a more immediate juxtaposition in the visual field of the spectator. Looking in one direction, Korakuen appears remarkably internal, even self-enclosed; looking in another suddenly reveals signs of its clashes with the megalopolis that has grown around it.

A similar type of visual disruption has motivated recent protests staged at the land artwork *Espacio Esculptórico* in Mexico City (figure 13). Created in 1979 through the collaborative efforts of Helen Escobedo, Manuel Felguérez, Mathias Goeritz, Hersúa, Sebastián, and Federico Silva on the campus of the National Autonomous University of Mexico (UNAM), *Espacio Esculptórico* consists of a large, circular field of volcanic rock rimmed by sixty-four imposing concrete wedges.

Like Tokyo's Koishikawa Korakuen Garden, *Espacio Esculptórico* invites its spectator to contemplate the deep cycles of time at its site. It also incorporates the natural landscape formation of the region: the uncultivated ground of lava in the center of *Espacio Esculptórico* registers the millennia of volcanic events that created the ground upon which UNAM was built and which previously made the area resistant to human occupation. *Espacio Esculptórico*'s frame of concrete structures is at once an abstraction of the urbanization of this land in the twentieth century and an invocation of the great architectural pyramids of the Aztec people, whose ancient capital of Tenochtitlán is located a little over ten miles to the east. *Espacio Esculptórico* is sited on land that is part of the Pedregal de San Angel Ecological Reserve, which protects it from further development. But in spite of this apparent safeguard, the artwork's viewshed was recently disrupted by the completion, just outside that protection zone, of an eight-story midrise building to house UNAM's faculty of political and social science. Dubbed Building H, this structure was erected without consultation with anyone associated with *Espacio Esculptórico*. In response, local sculptor Pedro Reyes initiated a campaign in 2016 to have the building either moved or removed, coordinating on-site protests and an online petition that garnered over thirty thousand signatures. Despite also gaining the support of significant members of the international arts community—who

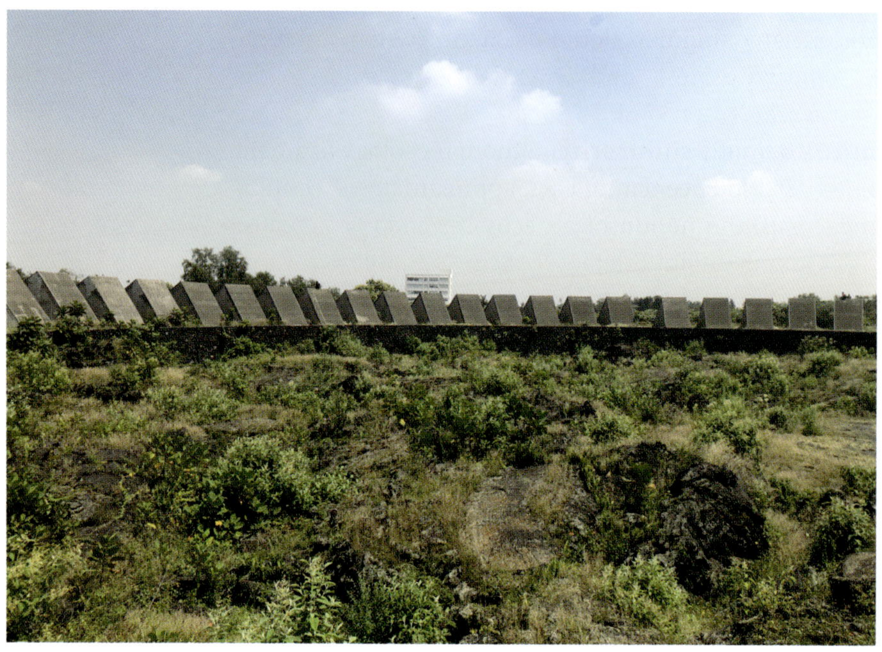

have promised to provide the money necessary to take action—Building H remains in place, and there are no apparent plans to alter it.

While we might bemoan the kind of encroachment exemplified by the Tokyo Dome and Building H (and rightly, I think), both demonstrate situations in which the visual field around a site took on unexpected elements, but in which the site's internal order was not intrinsically transformed. This latter type of alteration is more difficult to apprehend, because it doesn't present any singular elements, like new construction, to identify, protest, and potentially mollify. In other words, this other kind of change affects entire ecosystems. To briefly summarize, although ecology is a field of modern science dating back approximately a century and a half, the notion of an ecosystem was conceived considerably later. First coined in 1935, "ecosystems" initially designated interconnections defined primarily by the agency of animal organisms, particularly through the model of the food chain.[6] But following the conclusion of the Second World War and the rise of cybernetics, ecosystems were reordered around more robust systems theories derived from new computing technologies; the result was the influential paradigm of the "steady state." A steady-state ecosystem was characterized by a consistent order that was understood to be both predictable and unchanging over the long run of time.[7] Steady-state ecology remained the dominant explanatory model and means to imagine global connectivity throughout the long decade of the 1960s, when a public consciousness about environmentalism arose through such signal events as the publication of Rachel Carson's *Silent Spring* (1962) and the first Earth Day demonstrations (1970).

These basic assumptions about ecology started to be challenged in the years that followed, when a picture of ecological change as unpredictable and even chaotic overtook the previous assumption of unwavering stability. Longer-term studies led to scientists' realization that ecosystems do not have a natural and timeless steady state, but instead consist of a balance of relationships that are invariably altered over time by the influx of both immediately disruptive and more incrementally unruly factors. This revised understanding of ecosystems had an impact on another crucial concept in ecology: succession. Just as the word suggests, "succession" describes how one set of living conditions follows from, or *succeeds*, others. Akin to the concept of the ecosystem, succession was first articulated in the early twentieth century, at which time scientists had assumed that communities of species do not fundamentally change in the long run.[8] According to this line of thought, species might be temporarily disrupted, but they possess a natural order that will return if and when that disruption subsides. Following the decline of steady-state ecology, however, succession was likewise revised to recognize that, over time, species may decline, increase, disappear, or colonize to such an extent that they irrevocably alter the balance of their living environments, in one of two ways.[9] In a "primary" succession, an ecosystem arises in a previously barren region, and in a "secondary" succession, a new organization of ecological relations replaces a previously existing one. Drawing from theories of chaos, the revised notion of succession also acknowledges that such alterations are erratic and therefore not the work of a single design, regardless of whether that design was created by a person or by other means. In the words of the environmental historian Donald Worster, "'Disturbance' was not a common subject in [the] heyday" of steady-state ecology. "Now, however, . . . new ecologists [have] succeeded in leaving little tranquility in primitive nature. Fire is one of the most common disturbances they noted. So is wind, especially in the form of violent hurricanes and tornadoes. So are invading populations of microorganisms and pests and predators."[10]

The idea of succession is a provocative one for thinking about the ecology and temporality of sites. We might consider, for example, whether *Shift* has undergone changes so fundamental as to constitute a succession of its relationship to site. That is, have impacts on what was originally an artwork by Richard Serra, we might ask, been so extensive as to recast its site-specificity as a different kind of work, one less attuned to experiencing topological shape and more to grasping the complexities of change that occur within living environments? To suggest that artworks undergo this kind of succession, however, implies that the original intentions of the artist who created the work have been replaced by a different set of creative forces—which, in the case of *Shift*, are creators other than a single artist or designer. Artistic intention is particularly important when thinking about Serra, because much of the received wisdom about site-specificity in the late twentieth century in fact crystallized around his sculpture *Tilted Arc* and his stated intentions for it (figure 14). Originally installed in Lower Manhattan in 1981 using public funds, *Titled Arc* was cast in controversy following complaints from a few federal white-collar workers employed in the area; subsequently, a public hearing was held to discuss relocating the sculpture. Despite Serra's adamant testimony that moving the sculptural element of *Tilted Arc* was tantamount to negating its site-specificity and therefore the work as a whole, the sculptural element was in fact removed from its site in 1989, effectively destroying the artwork.[11]

Well before the *Tilted Arc* controversy, and even before he laid out *Shift*, Serra's ideas about site had been influenced by a 1970 trip to study the Myoshin-ji temple and gardens in Kyoto. On his way to Japan, Serra stopped off at the Great Salt Lake to help his friend Robert Smithson stake out *Spiral Jetty*.[12] According to Serra's later recounting, he took away from the gardens he studied in Japan a sense for how

> these complexes are organized with a rigorous mode of placement. . . . The articulation of discrete elements within the field and the sense of the field as a whole, emerge only by constant walking and looking. . . . This concept of space is essentially different from our western concept which is based on central perspective, and which arranges all objects on lines emanating from the eye of a static viewer.[13]

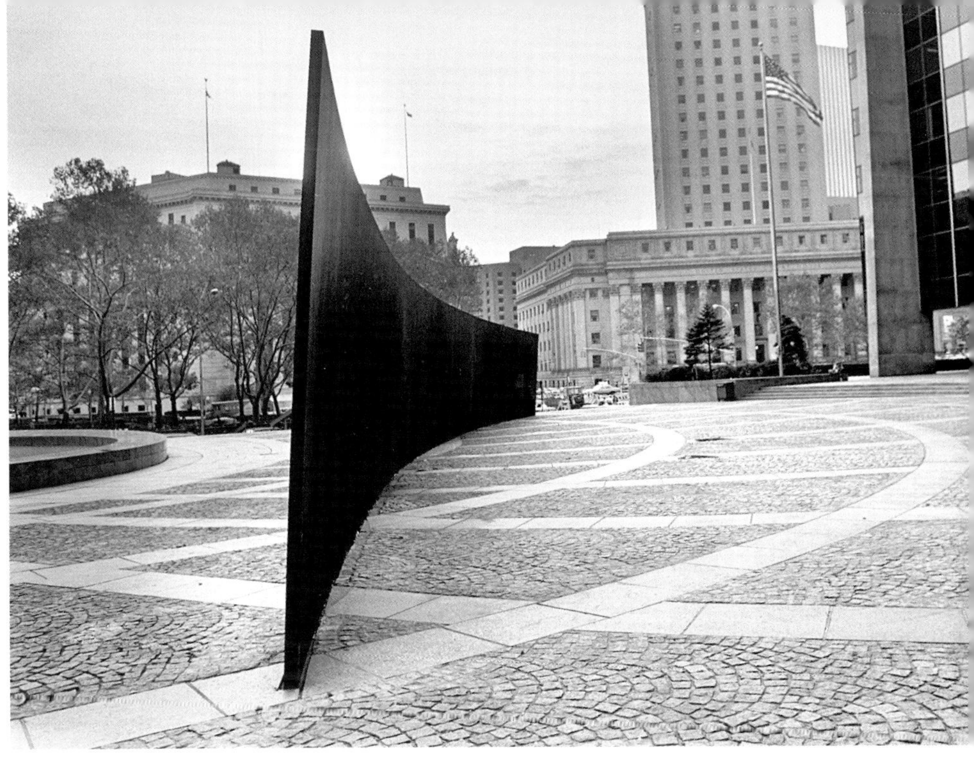

What was so significant—even transformative—about this experience for Serra was coming to this understanding that the organizational logic of space could and would only unfold through the act of passing through it. That is, not only was time important to experiencing the gardens, but the spatial experience of the place was fashioned by the time-based movement of its visitors. As Serra himself noted, this is a fairly radical revision to understandings of space in European and American artistic traditions, whether linear perspectives in the tradition of Alberti or the Cartesian cubic grid. Western art

Figure 14. Richard Serra, Tilted Arc, 1981, installation in Federal Plaza, New York, weatherproof steel, cylindrical section, 12' × 120' × 2.5"; collection of US General Services Administration, Washington, DC, destroyed by the US government, 1989; photograph: David Aschkenas, 1985

has long accepted that certain things, such as sculpture in the round, need to be walked around to be viewed in full. But Serra was not saying that the Myoshin-ji gardens—and by implication, his own later site-specific artworks—had to be walked through to be fully seen. He was saying that the work doesn't "emerge" until it is walked through. What I understand him to mean is that movement and duration actually *realize* the relationship of things to their site, rather than revealing a relationship that already exists.

Though dynamic and innovative, Serra's perspective nonetheless diverges from the concept of ecological succession with respect to what he further terms "rigorous placement." Succession disrupts any assumption that such rationally planned placement or design is sustainable within ranges of time that extend into the ensuing decades and even centuries beyond the afternoon of a visitor's walk. Nevertheless, as recently as 2008, Serra observed that the foundations of *Shift* continued to maintain the alignment of the work. "We had an engineer who took core samplings," he explained, "so that we could put its foundations as deep as they needed to be in order to sustain the load. So far it's proven to be correct."[14] Serra was also featured in *A Shift in the Landscape* (2014), a documentary film by Simone Estrin about the history of *Shift* and the local struggle to preserve it. In the film, he describes his conscious decision to treat *Shift* differently than *Tilted Arc*. Following an expression of gratitude for the "group of people in [the] township of King City that [took] it upon themselves to make [*Shift*] a permanent part of their culture," Serra explains: "I thought if I interceded on my own behalf, I wasn't going to prevail. I did that with the United States government, and it was a saga that lasted for about four years. It was very, very trying, and I didn't want to fight it out with the Canadian press." The result in King City was indeed the successful preservation of *Shift* as a heritage site, but to date no further action has been taken to maintain the work's sculptural elements. Whether or not those elements will retain their alignment or even continue to exist in the kind of landscape Serra originally intended has been left open to the more pervasive force of succession.

In 1978, the American artist Alan Sonfist created a work at the northeast corner of La Guardia Place and West Houston Street in New York City titled *Time Landscape*, which was meant to demonstrate the process and history of succession on Manhattan Island (figures 15 and 16). Covering a 45' x 200' area, it initially comprised three planting zones, each representing a different stage in the maturation process of the forest that once covered the island, ranging from grasses to saplings to developed trees.[15] The work took Sonfist well over a decade to realize. Having first imagined doing a series of "Time Landscapes" across Manhattan, he ran up against the reality of what it meant to acquire the

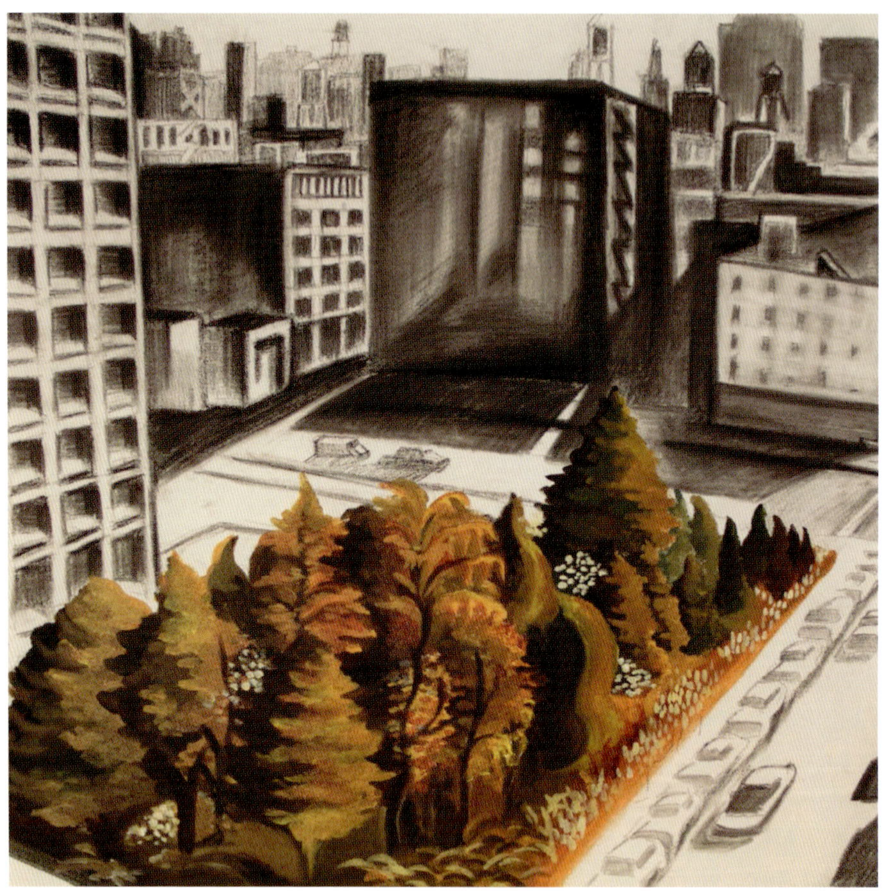

Figure 15. Alan Sonfist, Future Time Landscape, 1965 to the present, 45' × 200', New York, New York

real estate and funding to do so. In a written proposal from those early days, he framed his work as

a restoration of the natural environment before Colonial settlement. . . . Throughout the complex urban city I propose to create a series of historical Time Landscapes.

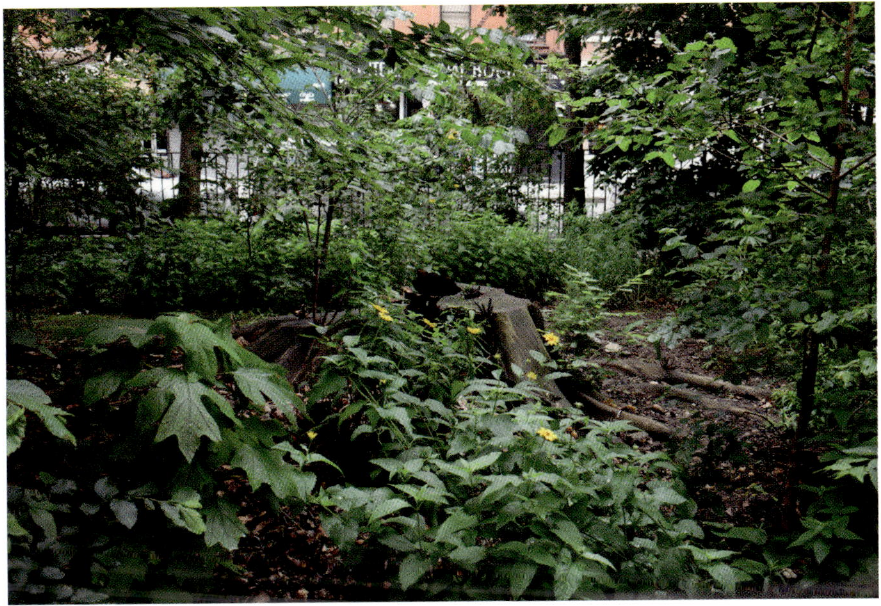

I plan to reintroduce a beech grove, oak, and maple trees that no longer exist in the city. Each landscape will roll back the clock and show the layers of time before the concrete of the city.[16]

In one sense, this is precisely what Sonfist did. The varying ages of trees and densities of undergrowth he planted at the eventual *Time Landscape* in the West Village succeeded in miming the stages of maturity that a native forest would undergo and had undergone in that place. He was able to incorporate dirt from beneath the city's original Dutch cobblestones that had been unearthed in

Figure 16. Alan Sonfist, Time Landscape, 1965 to the present, 45' x 200', New York, New York; photograph: James Nisbet, 2019

a nearby construction project. Sonfist also chose species, such as the red cedar, tulip trees, and dogwoods, that would have been common in Manhattan's pre-contact climate, before they gave way to the more northern species of trees popular with landscape designers in the 1970s.[17] In this respect, *Time Landscape* was conceived as a kind of reverse time capsule that "roll[ed] back the clock" to reveal Manhattan's native landscape across hundreds, if not thousands, of years in the past. Writing in support of Sonfist's project, one New York City Department of Parks and Recreation official described the work as "a developing forest that represents the Manhattan landscape inhabited by Native Americans and encountered by Dutch settlers in the early 17th century."[18] Such an assertion is as intriguing as it is fraught with the profound difficulty of unpeeling the irreversible clamp of colonialism to envision the history of Manhattan—whether as a grid of streets, a financial center, or a cultural hub. All of these elements of contemporary New York City carry the substantial weight of the dispossession and deep disruption of social practices associated with the colonial seizure of Manhattan from the Lenape people in the 1700s. Casting backward in the form of a park to picture pre-contact Manhattan cannot address the erasure of generational violence that such a fantasy would entail.

In addition to the colonial elision of *Time Landscape,* we might also consider what the work suggests about the ecology of site. Or what it might mean to picture Manhattan's arboreal succession in the space of a single plot of real estate planted a year after Jimmy Carter was inaugurated as president. Today the work remains in place, nearly forty years of growth having obscured the precise distinctions that were once visible among its three planting zones. While this is to be expected in the growth regions of a forest—even in miniature—other aspects of *Time Landscape* reveal the chaos of ecological succession more than the work's capacity for demonstrating an imaginary past. Although Sonfist wrote of his intention to create a landscape that preceded "the concrete of the city," the site's actual existence, marked by a number of anomalies that would seem entirely out of place in a snippet of old growth forest, has proven resistant to this notion. For one, the trees along La Guardia Place reveal a distinct phototropic pull into the empty canopy of the street, leaning into a space of sunlight framed by the midrise buildings to the west and south. Wind channeled between two condominium buildings to the south and east has similarly influenced the growth patterns of the site's vegetation.

Beyond such ambient effects, residents of these buildings have had a more direct impact on the site by hiring tree-trimmers to lop off branches overhanging *Time Landscape*'s exterior fence. Even more drastically, when city workers were recently called in to dig a trench through the northwest side of *Time*

Landscape—presumably to address a sewage issue— they severed the roots of the oldest elm tree on the site. This disturbance soon led to the death of the tree, which had grown so large that its removal resulted in further injury to the mature elms, one of which also died. Both remain on-site as large stumps. *Time Landscape* also requires regular maintenance to clear the site of rubbish discarded by passing pedestrians.[19] For nearly two decades, this task has been single-handedly carried out twice a day by a local resident of the neighborhood named Wilhelmine Hellmann. A retired electron microscopist, Hellmann also works on behalf of the New York City Department of Parks and Recreation to care for *Time Landscape*'s plants. Much of this vegetation remains from Sonfist's initial planting of the site, but Hellmann has also observed that the park contains a number of new species, some of which are native to the region and some of which are not.[20] Thus, to encounter *Time Landscape* today is less an experience of traveling back in time than one of contending with the complexities produced by the collision between Sonfist's attempted retrieval of the past and the reality of sustaining a small forest in the midst of an active urban neighborhood.

The Dia Art Foundation is perhaps the most recognizable institution that owns and maintains site-specific, outdoor artworks; it currently cares for *Spiral Jetty*, *Sun Tunnels*, and *The Lightning Field*. Each of these works has experienced its own vicissitudes in the decades since being completed. The *Sun Tunnels*, for one, have acquired strange, circular markings within the interior of each concrete tube (figure 17). Before her death in 2014, Holt surmised that these were traces of bullets shot through the tunnels, and, according to a current Dia curator, she understood them to be a part of the work's evolution that should be left untouched by conservators.[21] The experiences of *The Lightning Field* and *Spiral Jetty* are perhaps even more revealing in their respective differences. After *Spiral Jetty* resurfaced in 2002, Dia decided to hire a conservator, Francesca Esmay, to document the work aerially. In doing so, Esmay was attempting to track a number of factors, including water level, the drift of *Spiral Jetty*'s circular coil, and the buildup of silt deposits against it. While Dia continues to document these processes, it has yet to take any actions to conserve the coil itself. Esmay explained these choices in an interview:

> For conservators, when we consider intervention and treatment on a work of art, we often think about preserving "original materials" and strive to align any intervention with the "artist's intent." In the case of *Spiral Jetty*, both of these issues are not straightforward since the original materials of the object arguably began changing the very instant the artwork was completed. Therefore, citing an original condition to use as a benchmark for a restoration is very challenging, if not impossible.[22]

Notably, in deciding not to touch the rocks and dirt that make up the sculptural coil of *Spiral Jetty*, Dia has instead focused its attention on the viewshed around the work, attempting to preserve the appearance of the environment that visitors encounter when approaching and standing before the work. As a result, Dia has opposed local proposals to authorize oil extraction, but as recently as 2015 the foundation stated that it would not act to raise the water level along the lake's north shore surrounding *Spiral Jetty*, despite the sustained drought that has effectively marooned Smithson's earthwork.[23]

Dia has also resolved to conserve *The Lightning Field*'s viewshed by acquiring a land easement south of the work from local ranchers to prevent that land from being developed or commercialized.[24] Unlike its treatment of *Spiral Jetty*, however, Dia has subjected the sculptural element of De Maria's *Lightning Field* to more direct conservation, over time replacing selected poles that had been damaged by the local climate as well as undertaking a more significant and systemic effort in 2012 to reinforce the entire structure of the *Field*'s four hundred poles.[25] To understand this curious divergence in approach between one site-specific work and another, we might return to Esmay's criteria concerning "original materials" and "artist's intent." Given that *Spiral Jetty* and *The Lightning Field* are equally susceptible to changes in their environments, the difference between

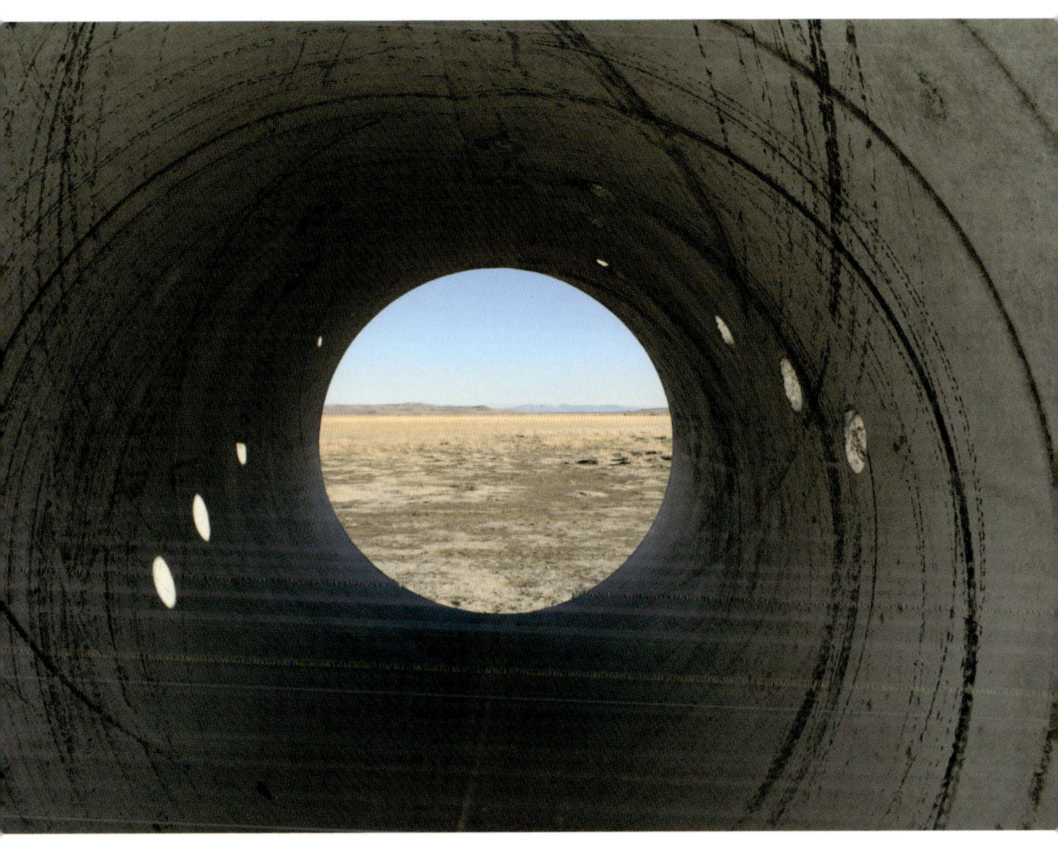

Figure 17. Nancy Holt,
Sun Tunnels, 1973–76,
Great Basin Desert,
Utah, photograph:
James Nisbet, 2018

them would seem to arise from the intentions of their respective artists. Smithson died in a plane crash in 1973 and therefore could not participate in Dia's more recent decisions, but he wrote extensively during his lifetime about his work. Across his numerous intellectually quirky and always studious texts, he valorized the concept of material entropy, which for him represented the gradual breakdown of recognizable form over time.[26] From Smithson's statements such as "nature does not proceed in a straight line, it is rather a sprawling development," Dia and others have inferred that the artist would accept the effects to *Spiral Jetty* wrought by the vagaries of erosion, coastal drift, and drought.[27] De Maria, by contrast, employed no such conceptions of entropy in his sculptural practice. He maintained extensive correspondence with curators during his career to repair freestanding sculpture that had been damaged during exhibition, and he even selected the particular stainless steel used for *The Lightning Field* for its resistance to oxidation rather than its facility in grounding the electrical current of a lightning strike.

Ultimately, however, Dia's different approaches to maintaining *Spiral Jetty* and *The Lightning Field* speak to the different relationships of these artworks to the organization. Dia was formed in the 1970s with the express ambition of funding and preserving De Maria's *Lightning Field* and similar long-term, site-specific works.[28]

Dia shepherded every stage of De Maria's project, from his first sketch of the work on a hotel napkin in 1972 to its public opening and promotion nearly a decade later.[29] Crucially, Dia was founded after the completion of *Spiral Jetty* in 1970. Smithson's construction of the work had been funded by his New York gallerist, Virginia Dwan, and was not acquired by Dia until 1999. Smithson never provided a long-term plan for the maintenance of his work, although, as Hikmet Sidney Loe has noted, the artist did submit a letter in late 1971 to Utah's Department of Natural Resources requesting that his initial twenty-year lease be extended in perpetuity in the event that he "should ever have to invest more capital to repair or restore the jetty in the future."[30] His untimely death less than two years later cut short the formulation of any such repair or restoration plans.

Recounting the biographical details of Smithson's premature death or of Serra's visit to Japan provides vital information for understanding their respective artworks. But these details also prompt challenging questions about the implications of ecological succession alongside the role of artists as individual creators. Can we really say, for instance, that Alan Sonfist is as much the author of the *Time Landscape* that exists in the 2020s as he was of that work in the 1970s? Or that *Shift*, both past and present, is solely the creative work of Richard Serra? What I am suggesting is not that Sonfist or Serra should lose their voice in expressing the significance of these works or what their future should entail. Instead, to fully internalize the implications of ecological succession for site-specific artworks we must also expand the time line of their authorship. If indeed the basis of art conservation is "original materials" and "artist's intent," then we likewise need to recast originality and intention as embracing their own kinds of secondness. With this broader and more dynamic understanding of authorship in mind, the primacy of Sonfist's or Serra's or any other artist's opinions about original intention should be weighed alongside other considerations and voices that accrue throughout the life of a site.

The very idea of authorship, of course, has been under revision for some time in art and criticism. In 1919, Marcel Duchamp sent his sister a geometry book to hang outside and be torn apart by the weather to make *Unhappy Readymade.* In the 1960s, Fluxus artists around the world more systematically formalized chance operations in generating their work. During that same decade, the American artist Robert Morris theorized a condition of unfinishedness in the materiality of his sculpture, a concept that he called "Anti Form."[31] In my own scholarship, I have sought to carve out a role for ecology in the composition and completion of artworks by connecting the role of process in Morris's Anti Form to emerging ideas in the postwar decades about the flow of energy through ecosystems.[32] I now think that position does not go far enough. To acknowledge that ecology plays a role in artistic composition is crucial; in Morris's case, such recognition connects his work to a range of European theorists from Umberto Eco to Roland Barthes to Wolfgang Iser, all of whom similarly sought to expand the source of cultural production beyond the preeminence of a single author.[33] Indeed, more recent interest in Bruno Latour's work on networks, Donna Haraway's on kinship, and the range of "new materialisms" to be articulated across the humanities has extended the idea of creation to relational frameworks that exist around and through cultural production. But in the sum of this work, duration tends to be limited to carrying out an initial setup or operation through time. For example, a chance operation may turn out a different result each time it is performed, yet its various results do not fundamentally change the nature of the operation itself. Even Morris's most radically open works, such as the use of steam as sculptural material, create experiences for their viewer that may draw on environmental conditions and even exceed the expectations of Morris as their creator, but they do not alter the process that Morris originally put in place.

Succession realizes a different order of secondness. Rather than creating unexpected or secondary effects, successions of site create entirely new relationships at an organizational level. At the site of *Shift*, these relationships have been forged by a combination of local activities spurred by real estate development and global events driven by climate change, just as a similarly broad spectra of local and global forces have generated new site-based connections at *Time Landscape* and *Spiral Jetty*. There is an important difference, however, between the state of these artworks over time and that of an ecosystem undergoing secondary succession. In the latter, the prior ecosystem is entirely overtaken, whereas in site-based art it is possible for multiple orders of meaning and operation to coexist. For instance, to visit *Shift* on a snow-laden day in winter or to view it from the air is to have an experience largely in keeping with the original work described by Serra. It is during spring and summer each year that a dramatically different work emerges. Both of these aspects of Shift can be seen as extant in the artwork as it endures from year to year, formed through decades of activity by a series of authors and agents whose collective efforts now exceed the condition of any singular plan or design.

Time Worlds

Just as the idea of succession underscores the systemic relations that site-specific artworks accumulate *after* their initial installation, so too does secondness require that we attend to the social and environmental histories that came *before* that moment. Robert Smithson, for instance, was deeply engaged with the momentous scale of geological time, writing in his essay "The Spiral Jetty" of a "consciousness of the distant past" and a need to visualize the "prehistoric world as coextensive with the world that I existed in."[1] The year before he made *Spiral Jetty*, Smithson and Holt had visited several ancient rock structures in Britain, including Stonehenge and Pentre Ifan, and a few years later Smithson praised "the Indian cliff dwelling in Mesa Verde [Colorado] . . . [and] Indian mounds in Ohio" as models of an unalienated expression of art and nature.[2] This statement was penned at a time when Smithson had increasingly turned his attention to joining artistic production with the environmental reclamation of industrially ravaged sites, and it reminds us that part of his attraction to the site of *Spiral Jetty* was the refuse he found there in 1970 from both previous and ongoing oil extraction operations. The juxtaposition of contemporary machinery with crude oil formed over millions of years would have reinforced his sensitivity to the earth's deep time, but it also veiled more recent social histories of the area.

Up until approximately the time of European contact in the Americas, the Great Salt Lake had been predominantly wetlands and had supported a centuries-old culture of farming and foraging. The Indigenous peoples who farmed this land were the ancestors of the Ute, Shoshone, and Paiute tribes, who would radically alter the use of this land by the eighteenth century with the introduction of horses and a lifestyle of hunting and gathering.[3] That no trace of these cultures was apparently visible to Smithson—or at least, was not remarked upon by him—is evidence of the profound effect that Euro-American settlers, especially in the name of Mormonism, have had in possessing and transforming this land since their arrival in the nineteenth century.[4]

The impact of settler colonialism—the eradication of cultural practices and the changes in land use—at the site of *Spiral Jetty*, as at any site, is vital to the work's temporality. In addition to the biological waves of change that characterize ecological succession, we need also to recognize the social—and more specifically, the colonial—disruptions of cultural meaning enacted upon sites over time. As the scholars Heather Davis and Zoe Todd remind us, "In gesturing to Indigenous suffering in North America we have great responsibilities to also attend to the time-scapes and realities of those people and communities whose ancestors were violently dispossessed through Transatlantic slave trade."[5] Taking up the prevalent notion that we are now living in a new geological age called the Anthropocene, brought about by human actions, Davis and Todd critique the dating of that era to such recent events as the great carbon acceleration of the mid-twentieth century, or the industrialization that began in the late eighteenth century, and argue for a "decolonizing [of] the Anthropocene" that would recognize the significance of the year 1610. The plant and animal exchange between Europe and the Americas and the mass genocide of Indigenous peoples that had already occurred by that date had a more decisive impact, they argue, on our current climate crisis.[6]

Thinking back to *Shift* and its proximity to the nearby metropolis of Toronto, a similarly decolonizing understanding of site would need to recognize that the very existence in the 1970s of a rectangular plot of farmland—a land area that was privately owned and made available for Richard Serra and Joan Jonas to walk and measure—was possible only as a result of European settlement. Prior to colonization, the land upon which *Shift* is located had been a savanna of mixed softwood trees, inhabited and managed by the Mississauga people.[7] The subsequent seizure of this land by the British irrevocably altered it: in allotting the land for farming, the British displaced its Indigenous inhabitants and significantly reduced the complexity of its local ecosystems. That Serra and Jonas could see across the apparently open expanse of this farmland to grasp its topography was less a condition of neutrality or absence—an empty ground awaiting the introduction of sculptural form— than a reminder of the past and persistent harm done to human and nonhuman ecologies at that site.

This discrepancy between, on the one hand, the seemingly uncoded status of abstract sculpture or the unmarked quality of a site awaiting construction and, on the other, the legacy of Euro-American imperialism has received increasingly global attention in contemporary Indigenous artwork. During the summer months of 2017, for instance, as part of the international exhibition "Documenta 14," Anishinaabe artist Rebecca Belmore placed a sculptural tent titled *Biinjiya'iing Onji (From Inside)* on the Filopappou Hill in Athens, Greece— directly across from the Acropolis (figure 18). Belmore's installation was inspired in part by refugee tent communities that she encountered at the nearby Port of Piraeus, as well as by her commitment to incorporating Indigenous perspectives in her work. *Biinjiya'iing Onji (From Inside)* is not site-specific per se—it was later moved to Kassel, Germany, and has since been acquired by the National Gallery of Canada—but the resonance it generated from its initial installation in Athens has everything to do with the specificity of that urban site. For like the Parthenon atop the neighboring hill to the northeast, Belmore's piece is also made of hand-carved marble, which was quarried from the same mountain as the marble used to build the Parthenon.[8] But that's

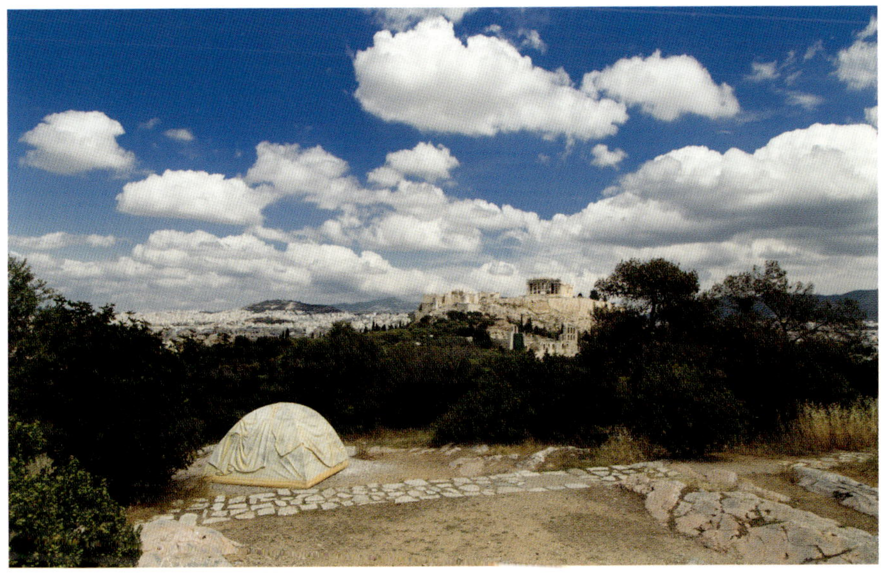

where the similarities end. In being sited to generate a dialogue with the Parthenon, Belmore's work was carefully fashioned in distinct difference, in just about every respect, from the presence and legacy of that towering edifice of the Classical tradition.

The Parthenon gives one a complete view of the city below, offering a perch of surveillance that slips easily into the symbolic gaze of mastery. Likewise, in its contemporary role as cultural icon, the Parthenon is dominated by crowds. Following military exercises of the Greek state that announce the start of each day atop the Acropolis, visitors quickly pour into the site,

Figure 18. Rebecca Belmore, Biinjiya'iing Onji (From Inside), 2017, Athens, Greece; photograph: Fabian Fröhlich, 2017

congealing in a matter of hours from stray groups into a single, tightly knit throng. The situating of Belmore's work, by contrast, on the side of its hill rather than on top of it had an effect of embedding her work into the landscape as opposed to rising above it. Her piece is also small and intimate. *Biinjiya'iing Onji (From Inside)*, as the name implies, can be entered—in fact it needs to be entered in order to be fully experienced—and it accommodates at most two or three people. In contrast to the bulging entasis of the Parthenon's vertical columns and its hard post-and-lintel lines, Belmore's work is curvilinear, appearing soft, like the folds of Classical drapery. But unlike the drapery of the gods and timeless heroes of Greek mythology, her tent invokes a more fleeting and urgent temporality. Its shape references the homes of refugees and migrants and is also, as Belmore has noted, "reminiscent of the wigwam dwellings that are part of my history as an Indigenous person."[9] For anyone entering such a structure made of marble, the experience is uncanny, for the thickness and scale of the material offer a quiet, calming, and, on a hot summer day, cooling seclusion that turns the very material of the Parthenon against itself. A tent versus a temple, *Biinjiya'iing Onji (From Inside)* is a personal space that juxtaposes a mass public one. While the Parthenon has long served as a monument to the origins of Western culture, the structure also stands as testament to the origins of the nation-state and its role in incessantly occupying and claiming new lands in an ever-expanding project to ultimately colonize the globe. Belmore's intervention in the landscape of Athens is one that prompts a profound turn inwards, against this other, ever-proliferating outward expansion.

The discrepancy between *Biinjiya'iing Onji (From Inside)* and the Parthenon, however, is also one of time. We might think of recent claims by scholars of Indigenous North American culture, such as Mark Rifkin, who describes a type of "discrepant temporalit[y]" in the relationship between "Indian and white forms of experience[ing]" place. For Rifkin, these "can be understood as affecting each other, as all open to chance, and yet as not equivalent or mergeable into a neutral, common frame—call it time, modernity, history, or the present."[10] To be in a crowd moving across the Acropolis might feel as though it and other similarly public sites are places of collective experience for all. These sites, of course, are not. But it is not sufficient to simply say so. In his influential book *Time and the Other* (1983), the anthropologist Johannes Fabian makes a claim for what he calls the "coevalness" of cultures.[11] Rather than explaining the internal worlds of meaning of one culture through the terms of another, Fabian suggests, we should accept that different worldviews can exist among groups of people living alongside one another at the same time. As theorists of Indigenous culture like Rifkin have argued, however, acknowledging coevalness does not actually strike at the specific impasse encountered by Native people, who tend to be understood as residing in stereotypes of the past or through the lens of criteria established by Euro-American society. In other words, the notion of cultures being coeval retains a false sense that these different temporalities of experience coexist peaceably, or, for that matter, that it is possible for one objective point of view to grasp and define them. For considerations of site, this means that any one location sustains a plurality of histories and significances, fashioning, in the evocative language of Marisol de la Cadena and Mario Blaser, "a world of many worlds."[12]

Although sites like the Parthenon remain touchstones for the discussion and critique of a Western society shaped over thousands of years, more recent figures in architectural theory and practice shaped the more specific understandings of site and environment adopted by the postwar generation of land artists. We might think of Ian McHarg, for instance, or the influence of R. Buckminster Fuller.[13] But to a considerable degree, the conception of "site" addressed by the first wave of site-specific artists can be traced through the seminal career of the city planner and architectural theorist Kevin Lynch. *The Image of the City* (1960), Lynch's first published book, is a fascinating read for its sublimation of the heavy grit and grind of city life into an ethereal landscape of urban images. "This book will consider the visual quality of the American city by studying the mental image of that city which is held by its citizens," Lynch writes early on, explaining that his study "will concentrate especially on one particular visual quality: the apparent clarity of 'legibility' of the cityscape. By this we mean the ease with which its parts can be recognized and can be organized into a coherent pattern."[14] This interest in finding and establishing patterns in the world would inform the foundational studies *Site Planning* (1962) and *What Time Is This Place?* (1972), which Lynch authored in the ensuing years. *Site Planning* is particularly notable for the burgeoning ecological perspective that bubbles beneath its surface. At its core, Lynch defines site planning as a fundamentally human activity that involves a "continuous foreseeable process" to bring an "original design, under the control of one agency," into a harmonious whole.[15] Against this spirit of control and command, however, there are inklings of other agencies that might already exist at a given site. "The site is a crucial aspect of the environment," Lynch writes. "It has an impact that is biological, social, and psychological. It sets limits to the things that people can do."[16] Lynch shows a genuine and deep sentiment here for recognizing the multiple meanings of sites over time, but for him these goals never stray from ultimately serving more singularly planned outcomes.

This inclination is perhaps most apparent in Lynch's last book, compiled posthumously following a heart attack he suffered in 1984. Titled *Wasting Away*, it stages a broad consideration of decay and its influence on human and physical environments. Establishing that waste is an inevitable, if not crucial, part of ecology, as well as a particularly acute issue for large urban environments, Lynch turns to a series of strategies for good management. Notably, these strategies include what he calls "waste art," which uses garbage and other refuse as artistic materials, as well as projects intentionally created to break down entropically, including Smithson's own works.[17] On its face, *Wasting Away* might appear to reverse Lynch's long-standing commitment to the central role of design in the systematic management of sites. For he does indeed suggest that ultimately such intentional actions submit to the same destructive forces that capture all manner of ecological structures and systems. Yet throughout he nonetheless holds on to the conviction that architects can manage this waste and ruination. This is to say that *Wasting Away* brings out Lynch's lifelong engagement with the issue of balancing the intentions of human design with the less predictable forces of ecology. Though his writing shifted considerably from the synthetic urban vision in *The Image of the City* to the more tempered position of his final publication, he did not shed the basic assumption that environments invite human control and custody. He did not frame these assumptions in his writing as a matter of politics, but they were largely shared by many of the first generation of site-specific artists, underscoring an outlook of conquest and possession in their work that is ultimately tied to legacies of land colonization.

As counterpoint to Lynch's thinking, we might consider *Reclamation Project* (1995) by the Anishinaabe/Ojibwa artist Bonnie Devine (figure 19). This site-based artwork consisted quite simply of a strip of sod that she draped across landscapes in southern Ontario. As Devine explains:

> I made Reclamation Project in response to the Ipperwash Crisis, an Ontario Provincial Police action against an Indigenous protest at Camp Ipperwash in the Kettle and Stony Point First Nation in September 1995, during which an Anishinaabe protester, Dudley George, was shot and killed by the police. In an effort to comment on the land claim and standoff at Camp Ipperwash, I installed six rolls of sod at various sites . . . for 10 minutes or so, just long enough for me to take a polaroid picture.[18]

The first site was a gravel road in the Lynde Shores Conservation Area, which adjoins two fields that are strikingly similar to the kind in which *Shift* is located in precisely that same part of the world. In another, the roll of sod adorns the front steps of a sizable health institute in Toronto. In each case, the ephemerality of the sod's placement served to highlight the difference in time scales of colonial land claims in present-day Ontario versus Devine's own *re-clamation* of such lands. As with Belmore's tent in Athens, Devine's work didn't

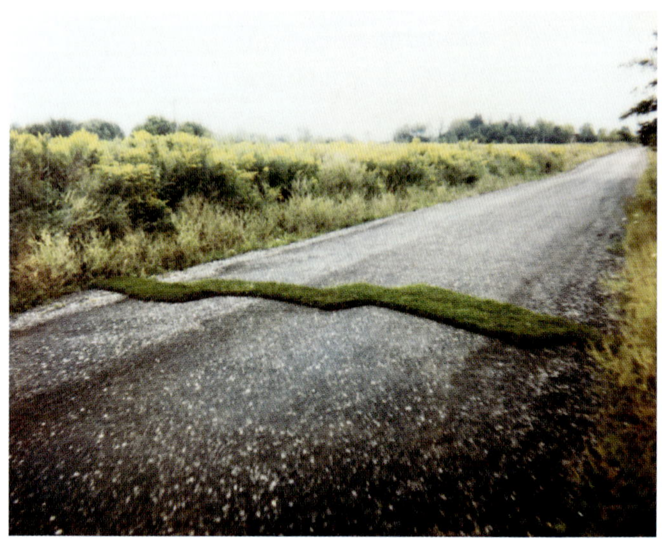

seek the status of being permanent to its site, which is to say, of possessing it through enduring settlement. These works of the two artists resist the notion that sites should or even can be possessed.

The relationship to site in their art might instead be understood through what the scholar of Anishinaabe culture Vanessa Watts calls "Place-Thought." This notion "is based upon the premise that land is alive and thinking and that humans and non-humans derive agency through the extension of these thoughts."[19] Place-Thought opposes containment, opening instead upon an approach to site always in a state of process and emanation, of being with an environment rather

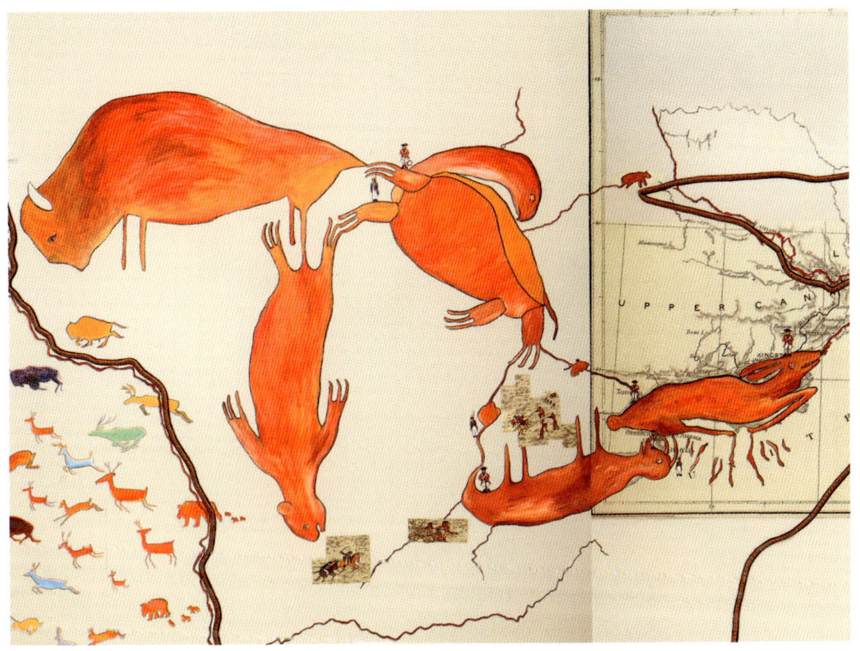

than attempting to own or design it. It chimes with Devine's description of her work as "articulat[ing] the delicate yet elemental relationship of land to consciousness," which similarly informs her recent mixed-media installation *Battle for the Woodlands* (2014–2015) (figure 20).[20] Comprising freestanding sculptures made from maple and willow trees and decorated moose and buffalo hides, the work is anchored by a nineteenth-century colonial map of the border region between Upper Canada, Lower Canada, and the United States.

Figure 20. Bonnie Devine, Battle for the Woodlands (detail), 2014, acrylic and mixed media on gallery walls

Over this map, which is cropped to include only two of the Great Lakes, Devine depicts the entire aquatic system of the Great Lakes as animals painted in red oxide—buffalo, otter, turtle, rabbit, and leviathan—in addition to showing clashes between British, American, and Indigenous peoples and placing beads along border lines once established by treaties that were later broken. As Devine comments, "I felt that no map of the Eastern Woodlands of North America should exclude its numinous and monumental heart, the life-giving waters of our home. . . . I pictured them as spirit beings, for that is what they are."[21] A final element of the painting shows dozens of animals fleeing the "catastrophic habitat loss" also caused by colonial settlement.[22]

Devine's approach to the history and reclamation of site offers a generative lens through which to consider *Dark Star Park*, a piece created by Nancy Holt over a period of five years, from 1979 to 1984, in the Rosslyn neighborhood of Arlington, Virginia (figure 21). Lauded at the time of its completion as one of the first permanent outdoor artworks realized with funding from the National Endowment for the Arts—in addition to funds supplied by Arlington County and nearly a dozen local businesses—*Dark Star Park* dramatically changed the course of a debris-ridden site that had formerly housed a gas station and a warehouse. Commissioned to accompany the construction of an office building at a narrow intersection of several streets feeding traffic

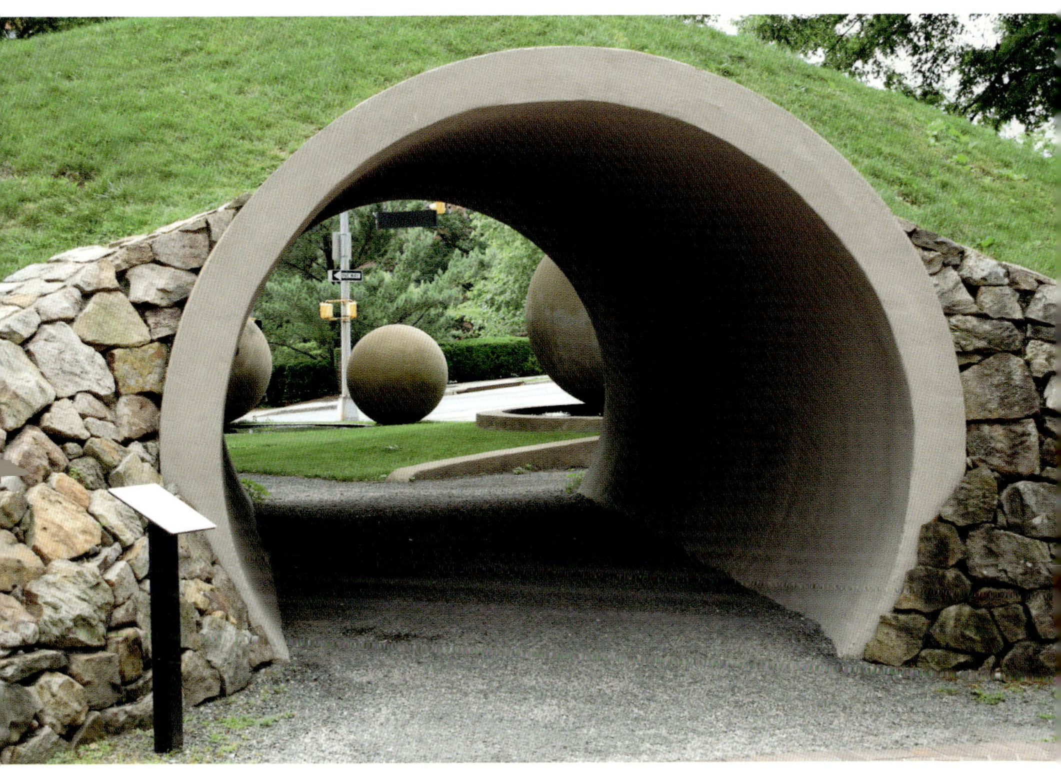

into nearby Washington, DC, *Dark Star Park* had been planned from the beginning as a site that would resonate equally with visitors on foot and those in cars. Comprising concrete spheres, tunnels, metal poles, circular pools, and vegetation, Holt's work is a complex sculptural arrangement that plays on a series of framed sight-lines that change with the direction and speed

Figure 21. Nancy Holt, Dark Star Park, 1979–84, Arlington, Virginia, photograph: James Nisbet, 2019

of its approaching viewer. Like her earlier *Sun Tunnels* in Utah, Holt's park in Virginia operates between the time of direct encounter and more permanent, celestial patterns. Specifically, the work includes shaped metal "shadows" on the ground that align with the actual shadows cast by the sun at the precise minute of 9:32 a.m. on August 1 each year. Thus, beyond its more conventional sculptural qualities to be experienced by walking through or driving past the work, *Dark Star Park* also embodies a cyclical time calibrated to the movement of the sun. While the artist's choice of 9:32 in the morning might seem arbitrary, the date of August 1 is a direct reference to the day in 1860 when William Henry Ross purchased the land from his father-in-law that would later be named Rosslyn. As Holt once commented, "By selecting that day for the shadow patterns to line up, I've sort of integrated the historical time of the place with the cyclical universal time of the sun and brought the two together."[23] In essence, then, this site would seem to be a symbolic celebration of both the founding of Rosslyn and its adjacency to the nation's capital, and also the recuperation of a formerly derelict plot of land.

But looking at *Dark Star Park* a little closer, we see fissures begin to appear. Physically, *Dark Star Park* hasn't held up well. Within a matter of decades after its completion, several of its objects were noticeably deteriorating. Its spheres, for instance, had been formed with an innovative technique that employed the sprayed gunite typically used to fill backyard swimming pools. By the late 1990s, these had cracked and been graffitied; similar damage had been done to walkways and exterior paint. Even more concerning than these surface effects, the water pools had emptied and required significant maintenance, while the metal-cast shadows, Holt determined, required more precise calculation to account for the wobble of the earth's central axis. All of these repairs were carried out during the early 2000s, accompanied by a celebratory rededication of the work and even a declaration of August 1 as the official Dark Star Park Day of Arlington, Virginia. What these various celebrations seemed to miss, however, was the more vexed relationship of *Dark Star Park* to the discrepant time worlds of its site.

Taking in the surround of *Dark Star Park* during a typical weekday is a multichannel experience. The internal elements of the work invite contemplation of framed views and the phenomenological experience of passage, but in addition, there is a constant and sometimes disruptive whir and rumble of car traffic, not to mention a steady stream of people hustling by to catch subway trains at the nearby DC Metro stop. Airplanes also regularly fly low overhead, on their descent into Dulles International Airport some two dozen miles to the west. Strangely, these planes are rarely directly visible; they appear instead in reflected glimpses in the mirrored curtain walls of the office towers that encircle the site. Rather than mere eccentricities of visiting *Dark Star Park*, these incongruous aspects of the work befit its internal contradictions. That is, while *Dark Star Park* offers a provocative collision of time scales that range from the urgency of commuting to work to the seemingly timeless astronomical alignment of the stars, these experiences should not occlude the violent disruptions and realignments of time that have occurred in the place where *Dark Star Park* is situated. In being linked with Ross's purchase in 1860, its composition was formed on the very basis of a colonial contract. How might we read this central aspect of the work? Does *Dark Star Park* celebrate cycles of astronomical and seasonal time as a form of gliding past and effectively erasing the more turbulent events of human history that have transpired during those solar alignments of the past four hundred years? Or does the fact that Holt consistently described her spheres as "fallen stars" suggest a more clear-eyed evaluation of the melancholy and foreboding that attends decolonizing considerations of site in urban American landscapes? *Dark Star Park* is a complex cultural object that offers no clear response. As one approach to reclamation, it has turned a disused, makeshift parking lot into a celebrated civic park; as another, it perpetuates and even commemorates the colonial dispossession of lands from their Indigenous inhabitants in North America and elsewhere. The bifurcation of these two conditions—or manifestations of "reclamation"—indeed realize a secondness of a different order than the type of ecological succession considered earlier. "Dark star crashes, pouring its light into ashes," the Grateful Dead had intoned in "Dark Star," first released in the late 1960s. "Reason tatters, the forces tear loose from the axis."[24]

The mutability of being situated within cities has proven similarly volatile for projects ranging from the dense metropolis of Stuttgart, Germany, to the more spread-out community of Amarillo, Texas. In 1993, the Dutch artist herman de vries cordoned off a small circular area in Stuttgart with metal fencing to create the first in a series of what he called *Sanctuariums* (figure 22). Akin to Sonfist's *Time Landscape*, these are enclosed spaces meant to be left alone, untouched by further human intervention. But unlike Sonfist's work, de vries doesn't mandate an anticipated direction or shape of growth for his sites. "The idea of sanctuaries," he has stated, is simply to be "a place for reflection, revelation, and contemplation amid nature's manifestations."[25] In Stuttgart, his *Sanctuarium* is sited at the tip of a small art park, at the joining of two busy thoroughfares, a site not out of keeping with that of *Dark Star Park*. By way of comparison, this Stuttgart park has considerably more noise and bustle than the city park in Muenster, Germany, where de vries created a later *Sanctuarium* in 1997 for the third iteration of that town's celebrated international Skulptur Projekte. Most viewers of his work in Stuttgart simply zip by in cars, with the intricacies of *Sanctuarium* wafting into their consciousness over years of commutes to and from work rather than through more attentive, sustained observation.

That is, this was the condition of *Sanctuarium* until the city unceremoniously razed its growth in March 2018, leaving only a patch of exposed dirt and closely shorn stumps. Protesters immediately gathered at the piece and wrapped its fencing with elegiac black ribbon, in support of de vries's statements published in local newspapers that the razing had "destroyed the concept" of his work.[26] Though Stuttgart's parks division initially claimed that, as part of a city park, *Sanctuarium* could be pruned at the division's discretion, the mayor of Stuttgart, in an about-face, later apologized for the cutting and invited de vries to stipulate guidelines for maintaining his work. From its outset, however, *Sanctuarium* was intended to exist free of direct human intervention—through maintenance or otherwise—and in a statement delivered in writing to a town meeting in August 2018, de vries advocated for the work to be reclassified and protected as a "monument" rather than continue to subsist as a park. As with ongoing discussions at the sites of *Espacio Esculptórico* and *Shift*, the future of *Sanctuarium* remains unresolved.[27]

Some two decades earlier, a similarly abrupt act had occurred in Amarillo, when the ten half-buried cars that make up *Cadillac Ranch* (1974), the iconic

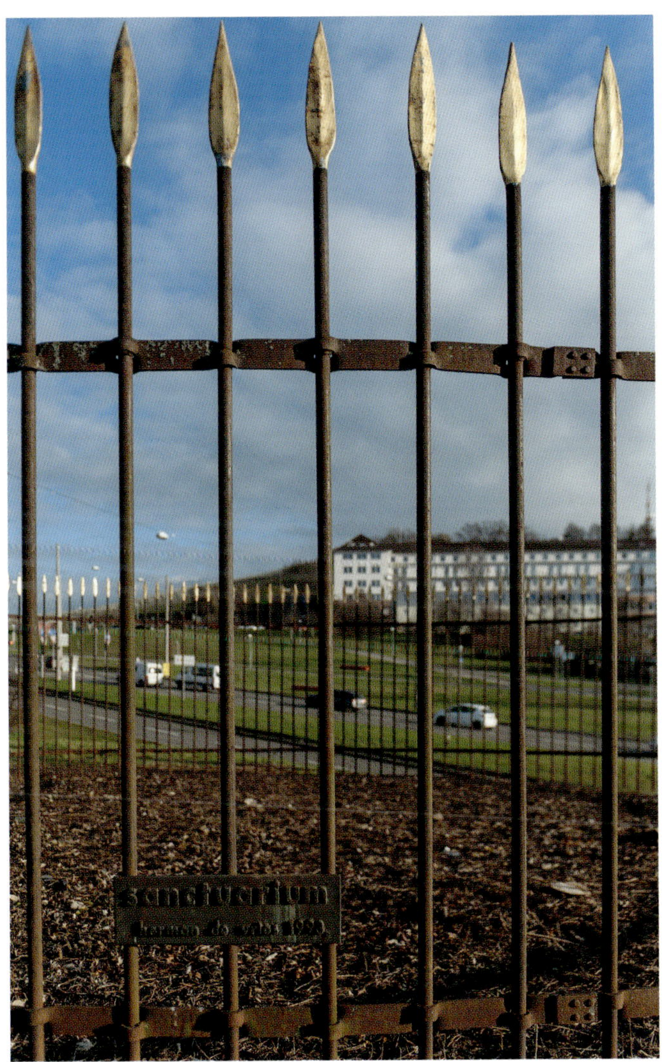

Figure 22. herman de vries, Sanctuarium, 1993, Stuttgart, Germany; photograph: Peter Traub, 2018

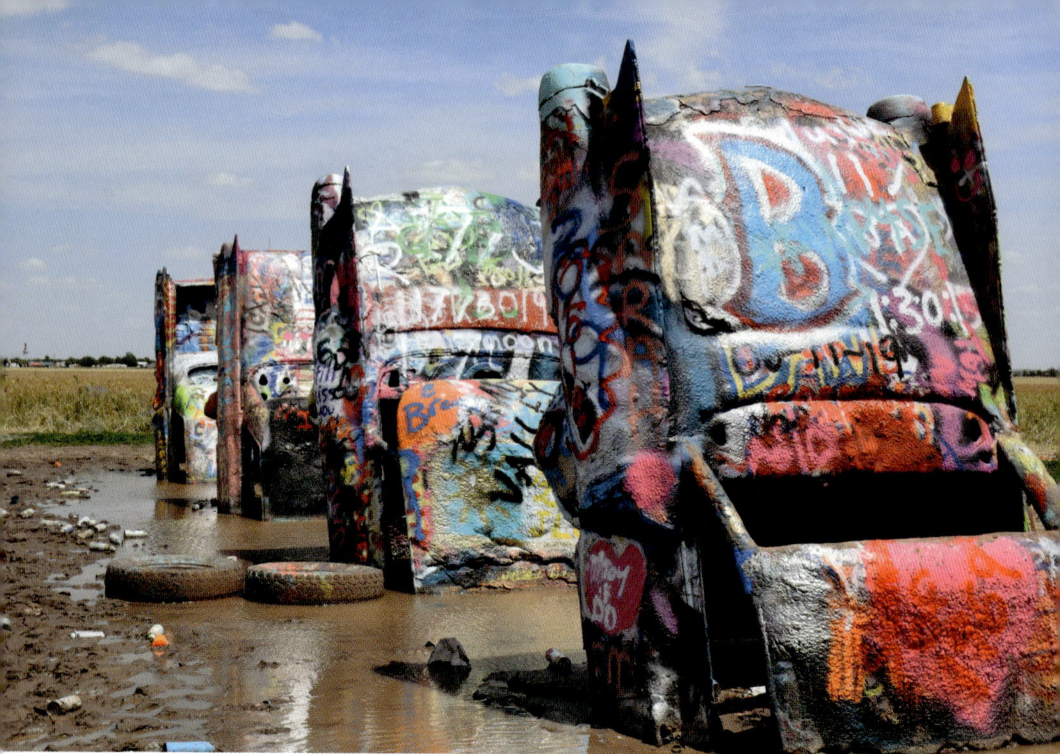

earthwork of the architecture and media collective Ant Farm, were dug up and moved two miles down Interstate 40 to accommodate the city's growing commercial footprint (figures 23 and 24). Today a Sam's Club sits on its original site. Since that time, however, what has been more dramatic and even traumatic to the life of *Cadillac Ranch* has not been the unearthing and reinserting that occurred in the span of a few hours in 1997, but the daily accumulation of spray paint that has come to define a more unique second life for this work than its actual second site would. Created as a roadside

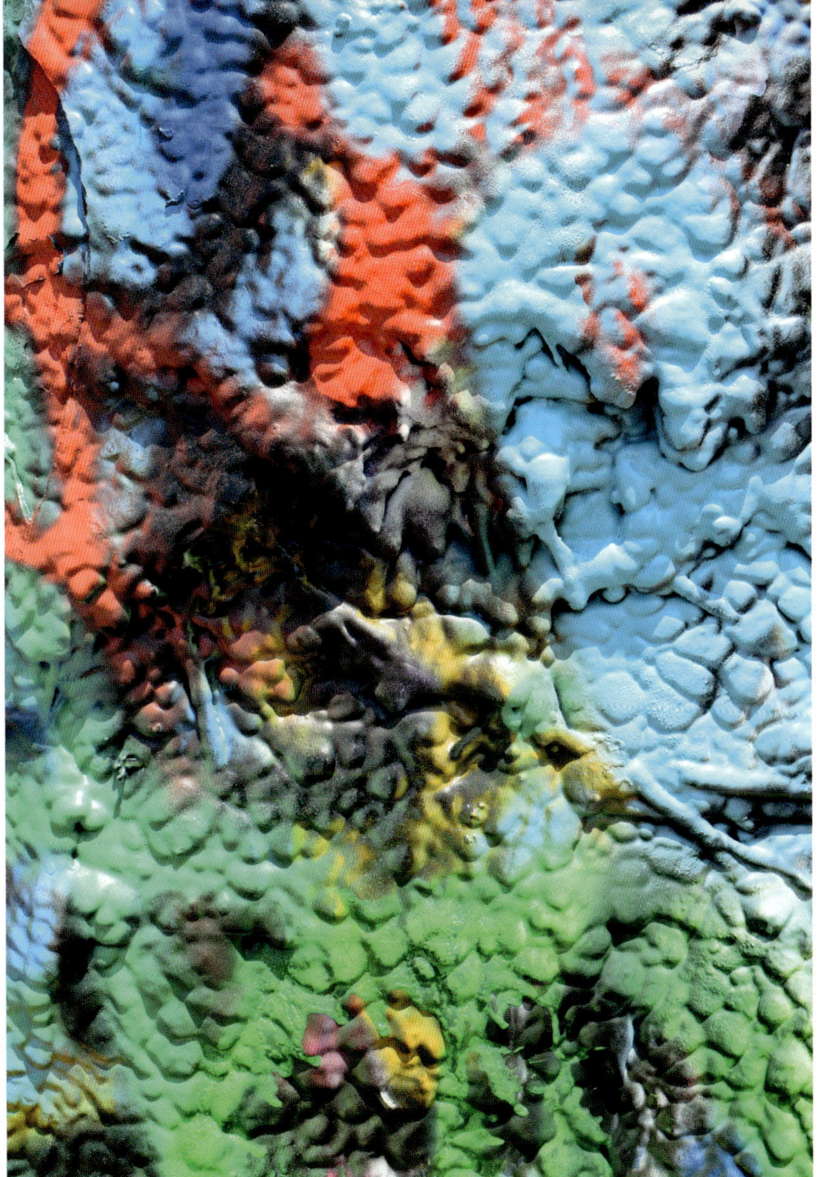

attraction after Route 66 had already lost its primacy as a cross-country thoroughfare to the interstate highway system, *Cadillac Ranch* is also a work of contemporary land art, a junk art sculpture, and a monument to the planned obsolescence of the American automobile industry.[28] The ten Cadillacs were buried halfway in the ground, in a row, headlights first, and in chronological order, having been chosen to show each noticeable change in tailfin design between 1949 and 1964 rather than representing one car per year.[29] Similar to contemporaneous works of land art, *Cadillac Ranch* had initially been known primarily to specialists of the art world, but it was later subsumed into popular culture after Bruce Springsteen sang about it on the album *The River* (1982). It then continued to appear throughout the 1980s as an element of what might be described as Hard Rock Cafe culture. By the estimation of Ant Farm member Chip Lord, the *Cadillac Ranch* cars had only been scratched with keys up until 1984, when the spray painting began.[30]

Jumping ahead to June 21, 1994, three members of Ant Farm returned to the work to commemorate its twentieth anniversary. For the occasion, Lord created a video that captures the small crowd that had gathered for the celebration, brief interviews, coverage by the local ABC newscast, and footage from the original installation of the work.[31] When we first glimpse *Cadillac Ranch* in the video's party scene, its row of ten Cadillacs

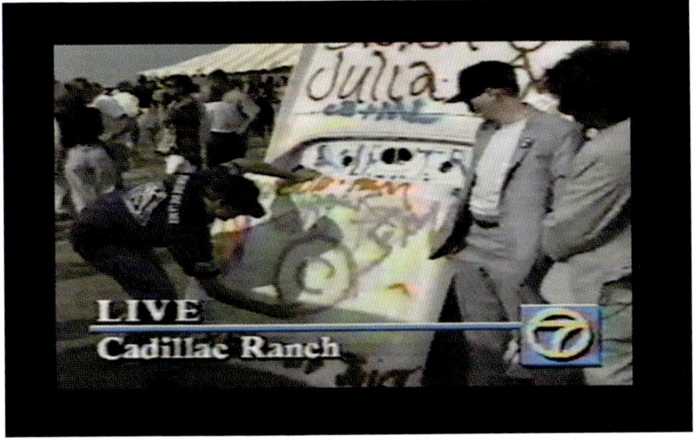

all appear bone white. They had been repainted for the occasion, like a ceremonial cake awaiting inscription. Over the course of the video we witness various participants scrawling messages on the Caddies with spray paint. By its end, the cars have lost their fresh coats and are covered with symbols, inscriptions, and indecipherable scrawl. At one point—presented from ABC's broadcast—Doug Michels, another original member of Ant Farm, draws a large copyright symbol on one of the cars as testament to Ant Farm's difficulties in maintaining proprietary control over *Cadillac Ranch*, which has been adopted by television commercials, music videos, films, and chain restaurants (figure 25).[32] In keeping with its location alongside the legendary Route 66, *Cadillac Ranch* was conceived in keeping with the lore of roadside attractions made famous by the Beat

Figure 25. Ant Farm, Cadillac Ranch 1974–1994, video still, 1994

generation cross-country travelers of the 1950s, but as Michels wryly comments in Lord's video, "A culture chooses its own icons."[33]

Whereas the first smatterings of initials and signs tagged on *Cadillac Ranch* might be read as a violation or defacing of the work, in time, as more people flocked to the site, Ant Farm decided to leave the piece unguarded and embrace its new condition. Despite visions among Ant Farm's members of "cars rusting gracefully in the field" and even "build[ing] a glass box around [*Cadillac Ranch*]," the work has been left open to creative interpretation by the public.[34] Four decades on, the cars that visitors now encounter are clad in thick, bubbling layers of multicolored spray paint. More than simply graffitied, *Cadillac Ranch* has become a site of daily overpainting. Some of this painting is coordinated, as when the cars were all restored to their original palette in 2002 for a publicity stunt by the Hampton Inn motel chain, painted black in 2003 to mourn Michels's untimely death, or arrayed in rainbow colors in 2012 for Gay Pride.[35] The results of these coordinated efforts do not last long. After each one, the work's anonymous painters promptly resume their efforts. The cars now hold inches of this layered paint, most of it banal clusters of personal initials, peace signs, and the like that have become so dense as to be largely illegible. The individual experience of *Cadillac Ranch* thus speaks in broad terms to the time worlds that attend urban sites.

Designed to commemorate a specific moment in the history of American transportation and middle-class identity, today *Cadillac Ranch*, with its wet, ever-sticky surface of spray paint, stands as testimony to how abruptly the specificity of local histories can be erased and enveloped in the activities of mass culture. The Cadillac, after all, was named by General Motors after Antoine de la Mothe Cadillac, the French colonial settler of Detroit. The remnants of overpainted Cadillacs that now sit in Amarillo attest to the erasure of this social history of the automobile as much as they do to the capacity of the *Cadillac Ranch* site itself to register the passage of social time, which is instead continuously overwritten and occluded.

Across town in Amarillo, Robert Smithson's final earthwork, *Amarillo Ramp* (1973)—which Holt, Serra, and the artist Tony Shafrazi completed following Smithson's tragic airplane crash into the site—is considerably more difficult for the public to visit but has been no less altered by recent history (figure 26). Most significantly, a dam that originally supplied water in a small lake around the work breached; as a result, *Amarillo Ramp*, like *Spiral Jetty*, no longer sits in water for any sustained period of time. Native mesquite "trees"—as the shrublike *Prosopis glandulosa* legume is commonly called—have also invaded much of the ramp's distinctively colored Panhandle soil, while the viewshed around it has been further altered by the appearance of

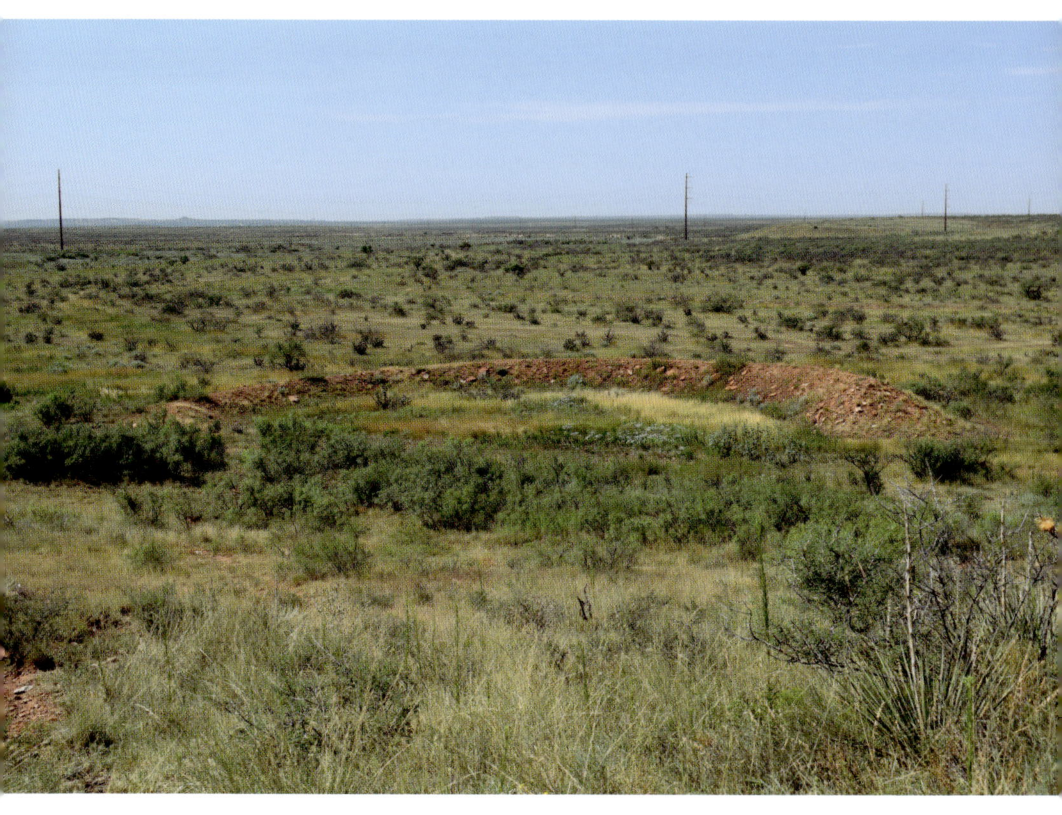

Figure 26. Robert
Smithson, Amarillo
Ramp, 1973, Amarillo,
Texas; photograph:
James Nisbet, 2019

power lines to transmit wind energy from nearby tur-
bine fields.

At the time *Amarillo Ramp* was completed, Holt and
Liza Béar published a succinct account of the work in
Avalanche magazine, which concludes with a remark-
able conversation between Holt and Sid Feck, a local
construction worker who quarried much of the fill for
Amarillo Ramp and operated the bulldozer that built it.
One portion of their wide-ranging conversation touches
on the importance of color:

NH: Have you been watching the light, how it changes
on the ramp?
SF: Yes, it changes colors all the time, every day. Now
you know, them rocks were all dusty 'til we had those
little sprinkles, and I noticed yesterday after we had
them how the rocks were cleaning up, and they're a lot
brighter yet this mornin' than what they were yesterday
evenin'.
NH: I see that they are . . . the rocks go through different
color changes, they can look red or pink or orange.
SF: When I ripped this rock I noticed there were different veins of it that were different colors, and I tried to
mix 'em as I put them on the ramp. Even when I got
'em out of my stockpile, I mixed them up for you just a
little to kinda change the color, not to make one solid
color on either side.

NH: Oh, that's something I didn't realize you were doing.

SF: You can see 'em on the end of it there, how they change color from the top to the bottom, and even on the side.[36]

Feck's comments underscore an element of land art production that Holt would foreground even more in later site-specific works: the collaborative decisions made between design and labor in large-scale construction. With the passing of time at *Amarillo Ramp,* the relationship between color and light observed by both Holt and Feck remains a part of the work, but with an important difference—such experiences of color, or any other formal aspect of the piece, cannot be so readily abstracted from subsequent signs of the social, biological, and technological changes that have encroached on the site. With every year that goes by, as its surface increasingly blends with the surrounding landscape, *Amarillo Ramp* is less recognizable as a freestanding artwork. Yet while new pockets of mesquite or the appearance of power lines might be new to the earthwork Smithson originally planned, the relationship of that work to the layered histories of the local environment is not. Unlike *Cadillac Ranch,* which has always been situated close to a freeway, *Amarillo Ramp* is located on more remote ranchland northwest of central Amarillo. Driving there takes visitors past, first, the

National Helium Reserve—a strategic holding of the US Department of the Interior that, in the late twentieth century, stored the world's largest supply of the gas—and then along trails that are maintained almost exclusively by the passing of ranch hands and cattle. The helium reserve is a marker of the US military's vast presence in the West, and the trails a trace of the settler occupation that forcibly removed Southern Plains tribes—Apache, Cheyenne and Arapaho, Comanche, and Mescalero Apache—from the region. Irrespective of the more recent alterations to *Amarillo Ramp*, these other sites have always been a part of the experience of visiting Smithson's work on the ground.

Thinking about the generational legacy of lands and landscapes, we might imagine versions of Belmore's *Biinjiya'iing Onji (From Inside)* addressing the elusiveness and multiplicity of sites across North America and Europe. Belmore herself has on several occasions created sound installations that employ large sculptural megaphones for speaking directly to the land and receiving communications from it in return (figure 27).[37] In this vein, we might also think of the signs that the contemporary artist Edgar Heap of Birds has deployed during the past three decades. Since the late 1980s, Heap of Birds has prominently placed written signs around public spaces like city streets, university campuses, and parks that name acts of colonial violence that occurred in these places and the Indigenous

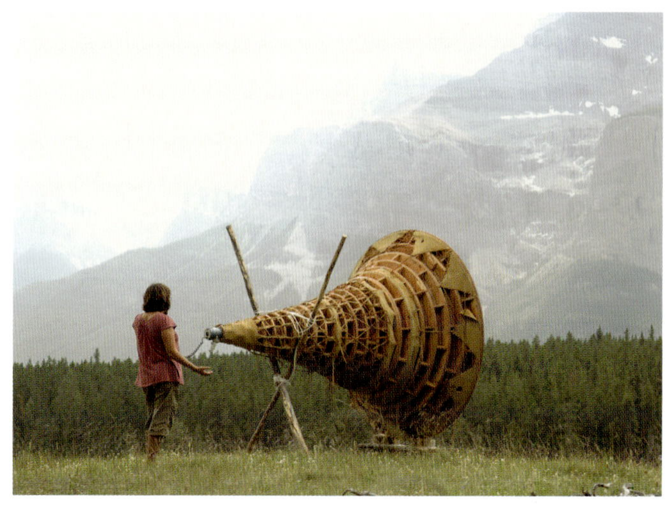

Figure 27. Rebecca Belmore, Ayum-ee-aawach Oomama-mowan: Speaking to Their Mother (1991), 2008, gathering, Johnson Lake, Banff National Park, Banff, Alberta, July 26, 2008; photograph: Sarah Ciurysek

Figure 28. Edgar Heap of Birds, Who Owns History, 1992, Pittsburgh, Pennsylvania; photograph by the artist, 1992

nations that previously maintained sovereignty there (figure 28). These "insurgent messages," as the artist calls them, challenge their viewer to counter the passive drift of temporal forgetting and the manner by which the inscription of power is written and rewritten within places with so little reckoning or recourse.[38] These messages instead insist on remembering the history of these lands, while not resigning their Native peoples to that past. Time worlds, invariably, accrue complexity. To think of site in this manner is to resist narratives that seek to establish points of cultural fixity, whether they be in places like the Acropolis or the plains of West Texas.

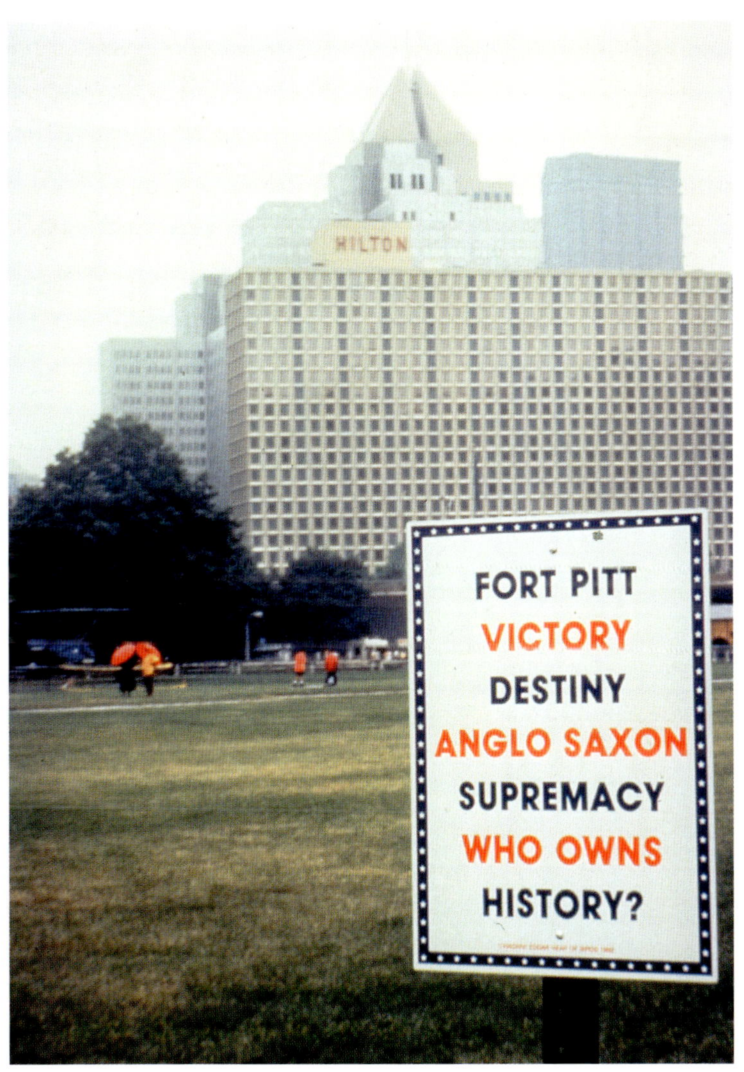
HILTON
FORT PITT
VICTORY
DESTINY
ANGLO SAXON
SUPREMACY
WHO OWNS
HISTORY?

Site-Images

When broaching questions of time and especially of memory in the flux of our living worlds, we might ask: What about photography? Or, for that matter, film, video, and the other recorded media that we so readily use to memorialize and recall the condition of places over time? Such media were very much on the minds of the artists who created the site-based works we have considered. Sometime around 1971, for instance, Robert Smithson wrote a short and yet remarkably sprawling essay called "Art through the Camera's Eye" that went unpublished in his lifetime. Taking on subjects ranging from conceptual art photography to underground experimental cinema, from the "Entropology" of the anthropologist Claude Lévi-Strauss to theories of urban abstraction, the piece extends a brief but striking meditation on the ubiquitous presence of cameras in the hands of contemporary environmental artists. In his characteristically arcane but unfailingly engaging prose, Smithson muses, "Physical things are transported by heliotypy into a two-dimensional condition. Under red lights in a dark room worlds apart from our own emerge from chemicals and negative. What we believed to be most solid and tangible becomes in the process slides and prints."[1]

What especially resonates from this statement is the internal rift or conflict it intimates. On the one hand, Smithson seems to be raising the possibility that entirely new kinds of understanding emerge through the process of photographic representation. On the other hand, he suggests that this same process reduces or thins the solidity of a site into mere "slides and prints." The first generation of American land artists held differing takes on the importance of photography to their site-specific work. Michael Heizer, for instance, displayed in gallery spaces photographs that were the actual size of his outdoor sculptures, whereas Walter De Maria, like Smithson, employed the pages of magazines and books to create original photo-based works that complemented his outdoor sites, rather than merely reproducing them. The many recent interpretations of Smithson's work and that of his peers have had a distinct focus on the role of photography.[2] Some of these perspectives remind us that the circulation of photography and film helped to broadly communicate his work to urban art centers, despite the distance of sites like *Spiral Jetty* from his home in New York City. Others have focused on the bifurcation or even trifurcation of photography in these works. *Spiral Jetty*, to continue with the example, is not solely a site in Utah that has been represented in other formats, but is instead, more capaciously, an intermediated artwork that exists multiply across the platforms of site-based sculpture, photography, film, drawing, and the written word.[3]

Like many of the outdoor works associated with

land art, *Shift* is also known primarily through its photographs. But in contrast to pictures that reproduce stable, two-dimensional artistic media like paintings on canvas, images of Richard Serra's work are closer to those of architecture, in their framing of space, and to unstable media like living sculpture or a deteriorating painting, in their capture of time. With the former, the photographer must necessarily select one or more partial views of the work with each shot; with the latter, the appearance of the work will change noticeably over the months and years between shots. These considerations suggest that catalogs on Serra could include numerous photographs of *Shift* taken from multiple perspectives across its more than four decades of existence in the world. These books, in fact, use only seven such photographs, all of which were taken in the span of a few days in the winter of 1972 by an Italian documentary photographer named Gianfranco Gorgoni.[4]

Having arrived in the United States in the late 1960s, Gorgoni initially turned the lens of his camera toward countercultural happenings like Woodstock. But after crossing paths with Smithson at Max's Kansas City, the preferred drinking haunt of the minimalist and post-minimalist cohort in New York, Gorgoni was invited by the artist to shoot *Spiral Jetty*. Although not commissioned by Smithson as "official" images, Gorgoni's photographs of the work, both from ground level and while hovering low above it in a rented helicopter, have

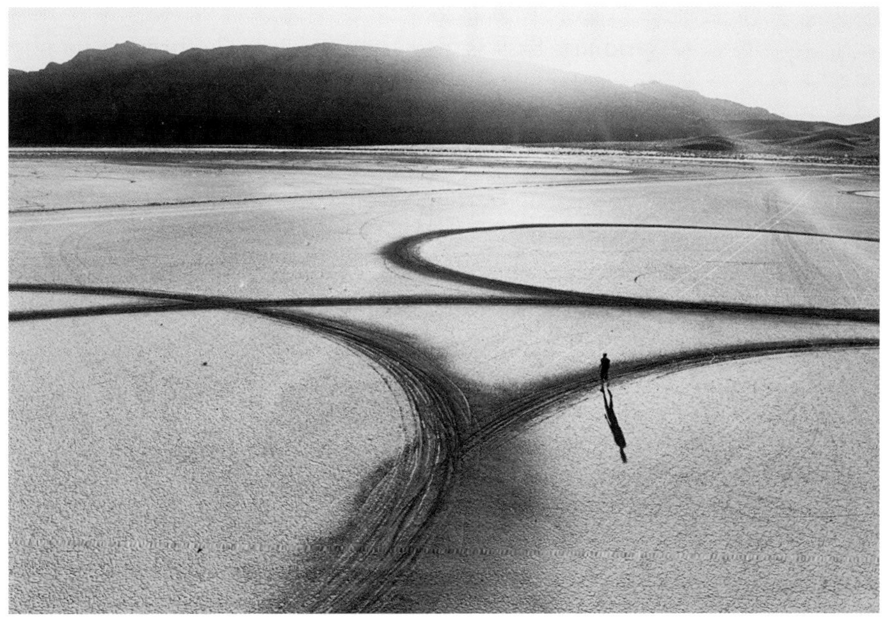

Figure 29. Michael Heizer, Circular Surface Planar Displacement Drawing, 1970; photograph by Gianfranco Gorgoni, 1970

become *the* most recognizable images of *Spiral Jetty*. Smithson, furthermore, selected them to illustrate his 1972 essay.[5] At approximately the same time, Gorgoni also encountered De Maria and Heizer, while the two were visiting Los Angeles, and accompanied them to photograph land art projects in the desert. It's Gorgoni's photographs that depict De Maria's short-lived *Desert Cross* chalk drawing, as well as Heizer in the raking light of evening walking across the circular drawings he made with motorcycle tires on Jean Dry Lake (figure 29). It was also Gorgoni who traveled to Amarillo to create the images of Smithson's posthumous *Ramp* for Nancy Holt and Liza Béar's *Avalanche* article, and who produced many of the earliest and still most iconic pictures of *Double Negative*.[6]

Gorgoni photographed *Shift* during a trip in which he was accompanied by Serra, Smithson, and the artist Mel Bochner (figure 30). Looking more closely at one of these images, which by its pervasive presence in Serra's literature has become the most common and representative shot of *Shift*, we see the work from a slight elevation afforded by another rented helicopter.[7] From such a vantage, one might expect a complete and comprehensible view of the work, but instead, Gorgoni's print makes it difficult to immediately grasp the essential details of Serra's piece. Appearing in places more like an abstract drawing than a documentary photograph, this image displays *Shift*'s concrete walls in a stark landscape blanketed by snow and marked intermittently by the meandering tracks of a few ambulatory visitors. One of these visitors, barely visible toward the back of the photograph, stands in a bulbous winter jacket and initially appears something like a small inkblot or smudge on the photograph's surface. Glancing forward in the frame, one sees heavily exposed shadows cast by *Shift*'s walls cutting further through the landscape, melding concrete and shaded snow into a sequence of thin, black wedges that do not lie upon the surface of the land so much as puncture and disrupt its seeming

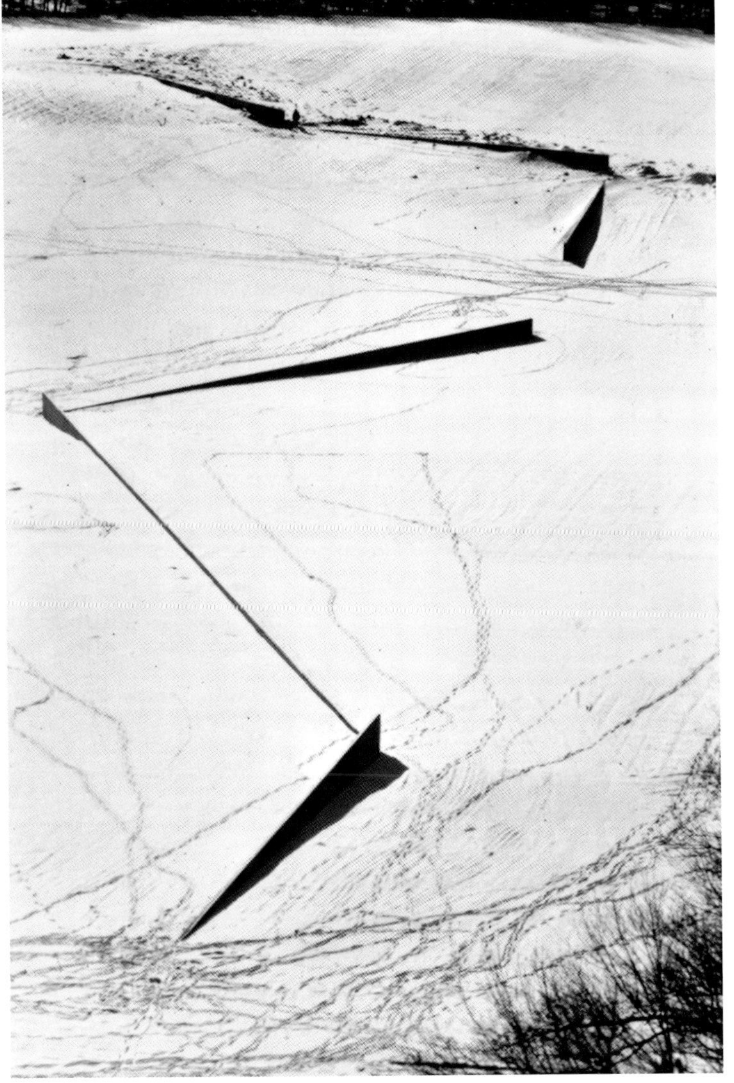

continuity as a plane of snow. Unless provided with the bare traces of orientation afforded by details such as the tree branches that seem scratched into the lower right corner of the photograph, or the hints of daylight breaking through the stand of trees across its upper edge, one might read this composition as entirely unmoored from a living environment, let alone an agricultural field. In this and additional views by Gorgoni that are similarly bleak and intensely formal, *Shift* seems to be abstracted from the unremitting processes of the place in which it was made and still exists.

This extended description of Gorgoni's photograph brings out just how unusual it is as a picture meant to document *Shift*. Although it follows certain conventions to isolate its subject—such as featuring only a single figure and depicting the piece in winter—the extreme contrast of black and white tones in the exposure adds a starkness to *Shift* that is otherwise absent in the myriad environmental conditions that attend its site throughout the year. Gorgoni's photographs of other land art works show a similar tendency toward seclusion. His pictures of *Double Negative*, for instance, show both deep shadows and isolated figures—most often, the figure of the artist—alone inside the piece. He tends to portray these figures as silhouettes—whether standing at the cusp of and upon the ramp of *Double Negative*, at the point of intersection between the long arm wrapping out of *Spiral Jetty*'s coil, or on snow-covered

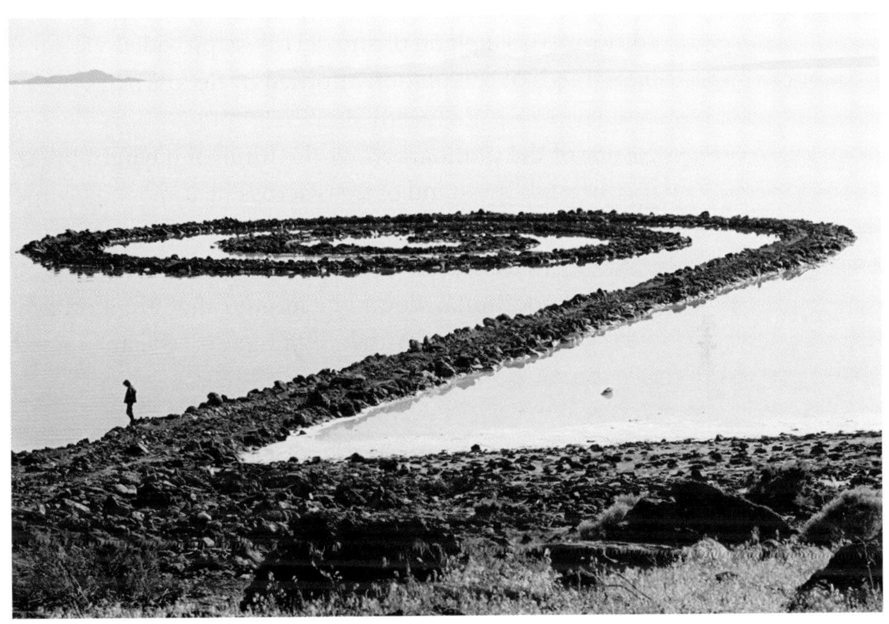

ground at *Shift* (figure 31). This to say that there is a kind of stasis in these photographs, as well as a focus on individual experience, as if subjectivity could be pared down to simply the motor faculties of the human senses. The visual language of these photographs is akin to the flawed fantasy of experiencing nature as pure phenomenology that has been dismantled by decolonializing critiques of ecology. Gorgoni himself, however, did not stop taking photographs of the land art sites he initially documented in the 1960s and 1970s. Although his

Figure 31. Robert Smithson, Spiral Jetty, 1970, Great Salt Lake, Utah; photograph: Gianfranco Gorgoni, 1970

historical images predominate in publications of these works, he returned to *Spiral Jetty* in particular throughout the remainder of his life, cataloging a range of new perspectives on the earthwork and its appearance over time.

Photography has long been understood as a "time-based" media, yet this notion of being based in time tends to refer to how photographs are made rather than how they circulate and propagate after their moment of capture. It is true that photographs record moments in time, and that this aspect of their production can be accentuated through any number of techniques, including long exposures, the use of serial images, and montaged prints that overlay images one atop the other.[8] But in thinking about secondness as a more aggregational understanding of duration, we might also appreciate how photographs enter into and become part of a site's ecology. In other words, there is a quantitative measure of seconds and sometimes minutes and hours imprinted in any photograph, but another aspect of duration comes into play when picturing places that so noticeably adapt and change. Individual photographs of these sites are less representations of what the work is, as a fixed entity, than visual traces of it within the current of its dynamic existence. They do not represent the work from an objective distance so much as they become material traces constituent to the ongoing life of the site. That is, photographs of site-specific artworks not only are creative expressions in and of themselves, in depicting that work, but also come to be folded into the mesh of relations and memories that these places acquire in time. Akin to a family snapshot, these images both are and are not the subject that they represent, at once embodying manifestations of that subject at certain moments while also casting it into a wash of memories and memorialization. Both internal worlds of their own artistic motivation and open-ended traces of ever-changing ecologies, site-images are integral to the temporal fullness of the works and places they depict.

In art history, it has become common for photographs to be described as a kind of "index" of their subject. This term derives from the semiotic theory of the nineteenth-century philosopher Charles Sanders Peirce; in art criticism, it was popularized in the late twentieth century via influential essays by the authors Annette Michelson and Rosalind Krauss, cofounders of the journal *October*.[9] For these critics, photographs act as an index in the sense that they imprint a direct encounter between a camera and the subject before its lens. In one of the most widely quoted statements along this strain of thought, Roland Barthes once declared, "The Photograph does not necessarily say *what is no longer*, but only and for certain *what has been*."[10] While Peirce did indeed make similar statements about photography's indexicality, he also conceived of the index as part of a much broader category that he termed, notably, "secondness."[11] Peirce's particular sense of this term derives from its place between his other broad categories of firstness and thirdness. Firstness is the pure perception of an environment—the raw unprocessed data of touch, taste, vision, sound, and smell—whereas thirdness is a condition of pure theory. Secondness is what connects them. It is an association forged between two things, whether as an imprint or a mode of directing attention. Therefore, it is right to claim that site-based photographs are indices of their subjects—that they represent them as a direct trace of time and presence—but such indexicality should not occlude the role that these photographs continue to play in the meaning of those sites over time. Peirce's understanding of secondness emphasizes the vital role that such images play in moving between experience and explanation—a process that, though it starts and stops at the moment of capture, extends into and becomes entangled with the expanded ecology of its subject matter.

During the mid-1970s, Nancy Holt began to experiment with the capacity of film and photography to describe a variable sense of time and place within a single body of work. In *Pine Barrens* (1975), Holt constructed a half-hour film that offers different approaches through which one might address the expanse of sparsely populated land in southeastern New Jersey named in its title (figure 32). Some approaches are visual, as in a section

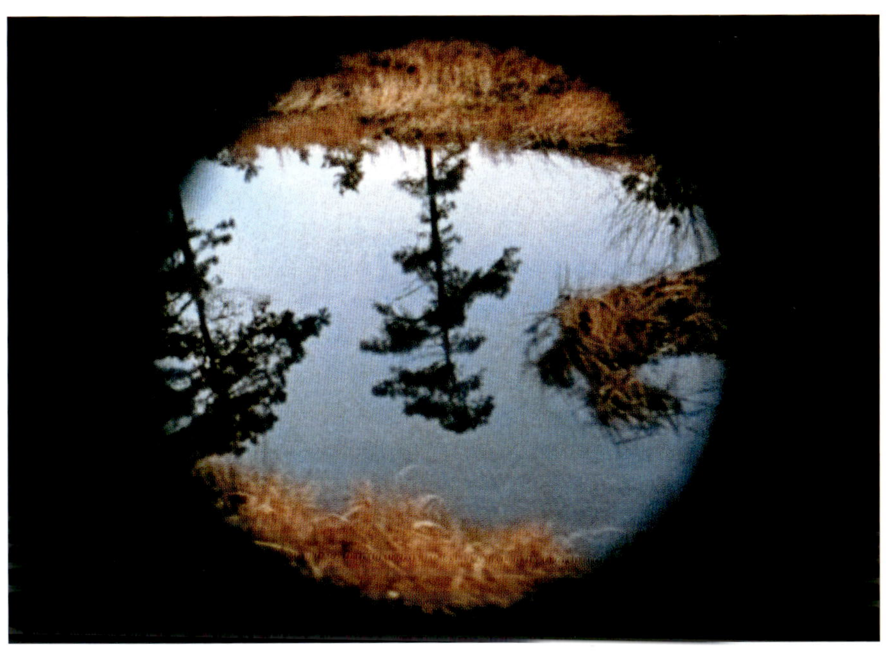

Figure 32. Nancy Holt,
Pine Barrens, film still,
1975

of the film that pictures the Pine Barrens as seen out of a car traveling down the highway. In another the camera slowly meanders through the individual trunks of pine trees growing out of the sandy soil of the region, while in yet another the shots are framed through a circular filter over the camera's lens—a cinematic device similar to the real-time framing of landscape enacted by the various tunnels at Holt's outdoor artworks. As the artist explained in a short essay about *Pine Barrens*, "As I shot, the structure of the film and the rhythm of the shooting emerged spontaneously from the landscape. The camera was always moving through space; the visual imagery was constantly in flux. Sometimes the filming was done from the car windows, sometimes I walked and filmed."[12] The audio tracks of *Pine Barrens* offer similar variety, ranging from an original musical score to stories told by the uniquely accented voices of local residents. What comes through most assertively in the array of these visual and aural expressions is the sheer diversity of the Pine Barrens. Not merely a site of aesthetic austerity or local lore, in Holt's film it is at once each of these things individually and all of them understood collectively as well.

If *Pine Barrens* opens up a way to see and to think about sites in myriad registers of perception, a video that Holt made on the occasion of the fourth anniversary of *Dark Star Park* pushes these different perspectives even further (figure 33). *Art in the Public Eye: The*

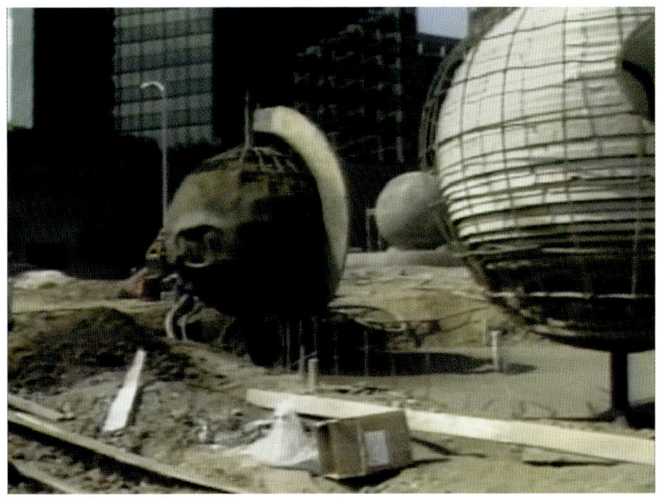

Making of Dark Star Park (1988) begins with a general description of the "trash site" that Holt first encountered in the late 1970s. "It had been a gas station," she says, "and it had turned into a parking lot—it wasn't even a parking lot—it was just a place with broken asphalt and weeds and broken bottles and where people were parking, so I really felt that there was an overwhelming need for a park here and I was responding to that." The video then turns to statements by the developer of the adjoining Park Place office building, the owner of the swimming pool construction company that crafted *Dark Star Park*'s gunite spheres, the construction foreman, the landscape architect—all of whom add to an understanding of the labor, expertise, and collaboration required to

Figure 33. Nancy Holt, Art in the Public Eye: The Making of Dark Star Park, video still, 1988

realize the completed site. "From working with people so closely," Holt reflects, "with the workers who actually construct my works, I realize how much art comes out of the matrix of society, out of, how simply, things are put together." Recalling her conversation with Sid Feck and the construction of *Amarillo Ramp*, the artist makes a crucial point here about the individuality of labor and its tendency to disappear into the fabric of sites constructed by teams of skilled workers. *Art in the Public Eye* also directly incorporates the voices of those who visit and sustain *Dark Star Park*—Holt interviewed members of the public who came out for the August 1, 1988, celebration, in addition to a member of the park maintenance staff. All of these voices, along with that of Holt herself, contribute to a view of *Dark Star Park* that pushes the piece beyond a singular viewpoint. Indeed, what most resonates about *Art in the Public Eye* is that it was made after the site of *Dark Star Park* had been in place for a period of time. The notion of "making" in the video's subtitle is shown to extend beyond the initial construction of the physical site, enfolding its ongoing formation of connections with the local environment and community.

By way of conclusion, we might consider one final documentary work. But unlike Gorgoni's or Holt's respective approaches to addressing specific artworks, Chip Lord's *Greetings from Amarillo* (2016) is a video essay that weaves in and around the site-based artworks that Lord and others created in the West Texas town (figure 34). Akin to the video that Lord made for the twentieth anniversary of *Cadillac Ranch, Greetings from Amarillo* is also staged around the artist's return to the site of his earlier work. But where the former centers on the individual history of *Cadillac Ranch*, the latter situates it within a broader sense of place. Structured around the time of a single day in November 2015, it begins with mists of spray paint being applied to *Cadillac Ranch* in the early-morning sun before fading out into eight subsequent vignettes, each named according to titles of songs on an album by the Amarillo-based musician Hayden Pedigo, which is also titled *Greetings from Amarillo*.[13] Through Pedigo's soundscapes of acoustic guitar and synthesizer and Lord's inclusion of occasional ambient noises, the video offers long, meditative takes of highway traffic, windmills, and freight trains, constructing a view of Amarillo anchored as much by its ranchlands as by a logistics infrastructure for the transport of grain and oil. Passing through a lounge whose walls are adorned with the mounted heads of ten-point bucks and a buffalo, pausing upon fossils of the sea life that thrived millions of years ago in North America's Cretaceous Seaway, and stopping by motels along Route 66, *Greetings from Amarillo* situates that place in precisely the kind of multiple and intersecting temporalities that have been the principal focus of *Second Site*.

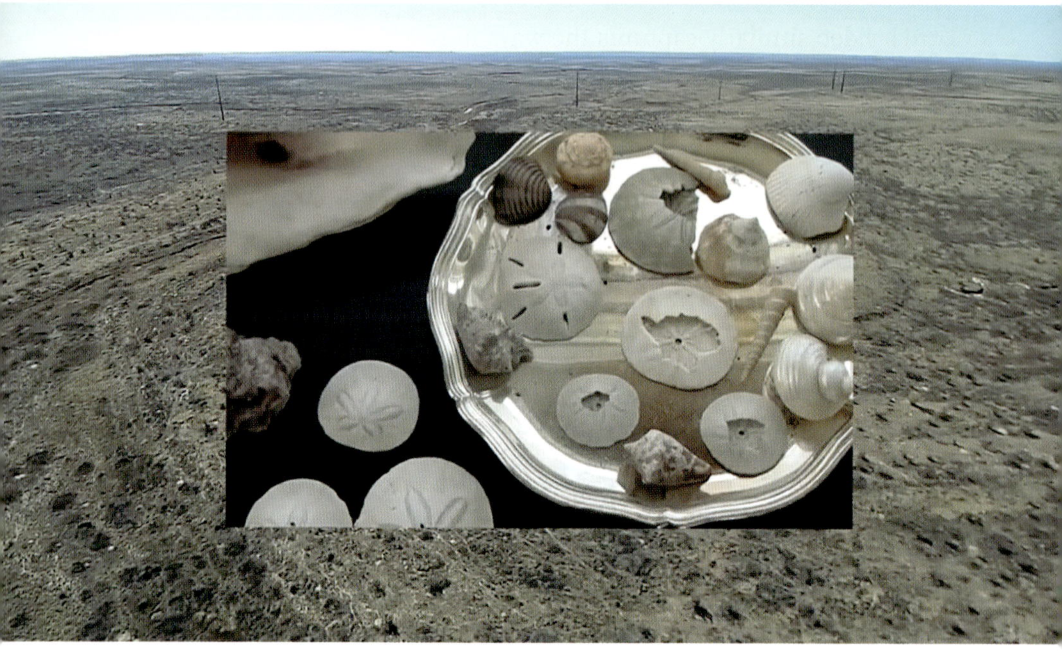

From minor modulations wrought by the passing spectators of site-specific works to major disruptions caused by environmental change, this book has considered the varieties of secondness that sites experience over time. Embracing the altered relationships of ecological succession, the radical displacements of cultural meaning encapsulated by the colonial splintering of time worlds, and the burgeoning flux of meaning and memory captured by photographic images, site-specificity cannot be extracted from its many past and future lives.

Lord's video similarly captures the ways in which Amarillo's changing landscape affects a manifold experience of time. From long tracking shots that underscore the bland repetition of new suburban houses appearing one exactly like the other to the suddenness and garishness with which highway billboards appear in the plains, *Greetings from Amarillo* employs additional techniques, including montage, freeze-frame, and shot reversal, to push back against any perceived singularity or naturalness to this place. Throughout, its use of picture-in-picture effects, with overlay frames that appear to zoom and ping across the screen, recalls early videos from the era when *Cadillac Ranch* was made, further emphasizing the distance from that moment to the present. In another sequence, *Amarillo Ramp* is seen from above; shot from an airborne drone, this view at once reminds the viewer of the tragedy that occurred at this site and the new technologies and amplified social surveillance that have arisen since Smithson's fatal plane crash. *Cadillac Ranch* appears three times in the video: in close-up at dawn, in close-up again at dusk, and once in passing, from across the interstate. All three scenes are vital, as they structure the personal aspect that attends so many experiences of site—in this case, Chip Lord was in Amarillo to check in with *Cadillac Ranch* and also to make a new work—without reducing those sites to the control or perspective of a single author. *Greetings from Amarillo* is a highly personal piece, but also one that is by no means centered by or on just one person.

It is crucial that the experiences of time that structure *Greetings from Amarillo* exceed any individual frame of mind or temporal measure. Ostensibly condensing the time of a single day into the half-hour length of the video, it also enfolds the relentlessness of commercial and industrial time, the constancy of wind and weather, and indices of deep time and colonial occupation. It includes glimpses of the guides and caretakers who sustain so many site-specific works with little or no recognition; in my own visit to *Amarillo Ramp* in 2019, Jon Revett drove me to the piece in the same Jeep Renegade pictured in Lord's video. Within the larger cultural environment of Amarillo, Lord's work recognizes that neither *Cadillac Ranch* nor *Amarillo Ramp* can be understood apart from the place of their making or, after spending nearly fifty years in the land, apart from one another. Between image, sound, and site, *Greetings from Amarillo* is a collaborative work in keeping with the collaborative and expanding authorships that site-specific artworks accrue. But it is also vital to note that the video is not an exceptional work of art. Unlike the singular and often monumental address of so many land artworks, including those depicted in *Greetings from Amarillo*, Lord's video does not draw its power from the originality of its form so much as from its more everyday manner of being and thinking. Unlike modernist forebears such as *Zorns Lemma*, *Greetings from Amarillo* does not invite us to see its medium in new or essential ways. Through a more unassuming style akin to a polished local television production, Lord uses digital video to invite the viewer to look past shopworn trappings of innovation and originality to instead appreciate the layers of accumulated form and historical exchange that constitute the site-specificity of Amarillo as a place.

While *Second Site* has addressed a variety of such specificities of site, in closing I want to be clear that these perspectives are by no means complete or exhaustive as categories. Against the grain of the many deeply rooted triads in Western thinking—from the triangle to the Holy Trinity to Hegelian dialectics—the three sections offered here do not bind in the same theoretical manner. Like any ecological system, the science, history, and media of sites are intimately and inseparably joined together, but their relationship is not closed to current and future alterations. By their very nature, second sites remain both grounded to place and radically open to ecological adaptation. They expand and endure through a combinatory process and logic rather than in series. Akin to what the philosopher Félix Guattari once called "eco-logic," grasping at the secondness of site is a process that "strives to capture existence in the very act of its constitution, definition, and deterritorialization."[14] As subsequent perspectives of secondness reveal themselves, they too should be aggregated with

those considered here, as facets that are complemen-
tary but never commensurable or reducible, one with
the other. As I hope to have intimated, the places that
I have discussed are merely a tip of the iceberg. The
attentive mindset and cultural conduct that secondness
invites far exceed any individual artwork or subject. To
embrace this condition we must embrace the imperfect
intermingling of art worlds and real worlds that attends
any site-specific artwork, accepting the sheer multiplicity and unpredictability that situates things and people
in place and time, which is to say, on site.

Notes

Preface

1. For a brief account of the sale and move of London Bridge to Lake Havasu, see Dominic Utton, "How London Bridge Ended Up in Arizona," *Express*, September 24, 2018, https://www.express.co.uk/news/world/1021814 /london-bridge-built-in-arizona-usa-world-lake-colorado -lake-havasu (accessed July 24, 2020).

2. On site-specificity, see Miwon Kwon, *One Place after Another: Site-Specific Art and Locational Identity* (Cambridge, MA: MIT Press, 2002); and James Meyer, "The Functional Site," in *Space, Site, Intervention: Situating Installation Art*, ed. Erika Suderburg (Minneapolis: University of Minnesota Press, 2000), 23–37. I discuss these texts and the art historical reception of site-specificity at greater length in James Nisbet, "The Ecological Site," in *Ecologies, Agents, Terrains*, ed. Christopher P. Heuer and Rebecca Zorach (Williamstown, MA, and New Haven, CT: Clark Art Institute and Yale University Press, 2018), 3–33.

3. On the international range of land art practices, see Philipp Kaiser and Miwon Kwon's excellent catalog, *Ends of the Earth: Land Art to 1974* (exhibition catalog) (Los Angeles: Museum of Contemporary Art, 2012). Additional overviews of the movement can be found in John Beardsley, *Earthworks and Beyond: Contemporary Art in the Landscape*, 4th ed. (New York: Abbeville Press, 2006); and Suzaan Boettger, *Earthworks: Art and the Landscape of the Sixties* (Berkeley: University of California Press, 2002).

4. For further analysis and critique of the historical constructions of the American desert, see Lyle Massey and James Nisbet, eds., *The Invention of the American Desert: Art, Land, and the Politics of Environment* (Berkeley: University of California Press, 2021).

5. Ecological interpretations of art history and visual culture have developed significantly in the past decade. Without attempting to summarize that entire body of literature, I would note that when I wrote *Ecologies, Environments, and Energy Systems in Art of the 1960s and 1970s* (Cambridge, MA: MIT Press, 2014), there were very few dedicated studies in the field that addressed issues of ecology, as distinct from more conventional subjects such as landscape or the natural environment. Since that time, ecological perspectives have emerged as central to thinking about historical questions in the discipline, as well as contemporary issues such climate crisis, environmental racism, and animal rights. For a notable selection of this emerging scholarship in reverse chronology, see Amanda Boetzkes, *Plastic Capitalism: Contemporary Art and the Drive to Waste* (Cambridge, MA: MIT Press, 2019); Sugata Ray, *Climate Change and the Art of Devotion: Geoaesthetics in the Land of Krishna, 1550–1850* (Seattle: University of Washington Press, 2019); Mark A. Cheetham, *Landscape into Eco Art: Articulations of Nature since the '60s* (University Park: Pennsylvania State University Press, 2018); Christopher P. Heuer and Rebecca Zorach, eds., *Ecologies, Agents, Terrains* (Williamstown, MA, and New Haven, CT: Clark Art Institute and Yale University Press, 2018); Jessica L. Horton, *Art for an Undivided Earth: The American Indian Movement Generation* (Durham, NC: Duke University Press, 2017); T. J. Demos, *Decolonizing*

Nature: Contemporary Art and the Politics of Ecology
(New York: Sternberg, 2016); and Emily Eliza Scott and
Kirsten J. Swenson, *Critical Landscapes: Art, Space, Politics*
(Berkeley: University of California Press, 2015). For a
critical overview, see Alan C. Braddock, "From Nature to
Ecology: The Emergence of Ecocritical Art History," in
A Companion to American Art, ed. John Davis, Jennifer A.
Greenhill, and Jason D. LaFountain (Hoboken, NJ: Wiley
and Sons, 2015), 447–67.

6. The term *longue durée* was established by the Annales
school of French historians in the twentieth century to
focus on long-term vehicles of historical change rather
than influential individuals or events. I invoke the term
longue durée here to shift that mode of thinking to encompass the environmental impact of duration, in addition to
that of social structures.

7. Two recent publications that not only address the
historiography of temporal theories of art but also add
new perspectives include Dan Karlholm and Keith Moxey,
eds., *Time in the History of Art: Temporality, Chronology, and Anachrony* (New York: Routledge, 2018); and
Christine Ross, *The Past Is the Present; It's the Future
Too: The Temporal Turn in Contemporary Art* (New York:
Continuum, 2012). Ross's chapter on "Ecology" differs
from my own approach in that it employs this term to
describe a mode of awareness wherein "the subject is
made to be perceptually attuned with his or her environment instead of being detached from it" (65). *The Shape
of Time: Remarks on the History of Things* by George Kubler
(New Haven, CT: Yale University Press, 1962) is also
an important touchstone for its adoption of ideas from
the natural and physical sciences into discussions of art

historical methodology. Another body of work that has been influential analyzes and critiques cultures of instantaneity, including Jonathan Crary, *24/7: Late Capitalism and the Ends of Sleep* (New York: Verso, 2014); Paul Virilio, *The Vision Machine*, trans. Julie Rose (Bloomington: Indiana University Press, 1994); and T. J. Demos's work-in-progress, "Radical Futurisms: Ecologies of Collapse/Chronopolitics/Justice to Come."

8. Raymond Williams, "Ideas of Nature," in *Ecology: The Shaping Enquiry*, ed. Jonathan Benthall (London: Longman, 1972), 146–64.

9. During the late 1860s and early 1870s, Maxwell imagined the "demon" of his thought experiment as an intentionally absurd exception to the Second Law of Thermodynamics, which holds that two bodies brought into contact will reach thermodynamic equilibrium as the entropy within that joint system increases. Guarding the passage between two chambers filled with gas, Maxwell's demon would allow only molecules in a higher state of excitation to pass in one direction and less energetic molecules to move in the other, resulting in one chamber with a monopoly of energy over the other. On Frampton's film *Maxwell's Demon*, see Daniel Hackbarth and James Nisbet, "Photography as Photoenergy," in *Energies in the Arts*, ed. Douglas Kahn (Cambridge, MA: MIT Press, 2019), 87–126.

10. Zorn's lemma is a mathematical principle that describes the existence of a maximum element in a given set when that element cannot be shown to exist on its own. Since the Polish mathematician Kazimierz

Kuratowski had earlier discovered the same principle in 1922, it is also called the Kuratowski-Zorn lemma.

11. Mohsen Mostafavi and David Leatherbarrow, *On Weathering: The Life of Buildings in Time* (Cambridge, MA: MIT Press, 1993).

12. On Holt's larger body of artwork, see *Nancy Holt: Sightlines* (exhibition catalog), ed. Alena J. Williams (Berkeley: University of California Press, 2011), in addition to the scholarly texts published on the website of the Holt/Smithson Foundation, https://holtsmith sonfoundation.org/scholarly-texts (accessed January 18, 2021).

13. On the commission and conservation of the Tampere region land art sites, see Eero Yli-Vakkuri, "On Land and Environmental Art Conservation," in *Crossroads: New Views on Art and Environment*, ed. Ilari Laamanen (New York and Helsinki: Finnish Cultural Institute and University of the Arts, 2019), 118–34. For an excellent overview of Finnish environmental art, see Hanna Johansson's essay "The Nature of (Finnish) Earth Art: Crossing Paths and Temporal Transitions" in the same volume (44–69).

14. Agnes Denes, "Notes on Eco-Logic: Environmental Artwork, Visual Philosophy, and Global Perspective," *Leonardo* 26, no. 5 (1993): 391.

15. Arthur Danto, "The Artworld," *Journal of Philosophy* 61, no. 19 (October 15, 1964): 582.

16. Alfred Gell, "Vogel's Net: Traps as Artworks and Artworks as Traps," *Journal of Material Culture* 1, no. 1 (1996): 15–38.

17. The term "secondness" is most closely associated with the philosopher Charles Sanders Peirce. As I discuss in more detail in "Site-Images," my use of secondness intersects with that of Peirce, but carries different meanings in other parts of *Second Site* that pertain to specifically ecological perspectives on alteration and temporality.

18. Some of the "wildfires" currently being exacerbated by the earth's ever more extreme climate are intentionally started and some are not; the Presidio fire was most likely caused, according to local reporting, by arson. See Brett Simpson, Emily Fancher, and Sam Whiting, "Arson Suspected in Fire That Damaged 'Spire' Sculpture in San Francisco's Presidio," *San Francisco Chronicle*, June 23, 2020, https://www.sfchronicle.com/bayarea/article/Fires-in-San-Francisco-s-Presidio-threaten-15360113.php (accessed July 24, 2020).

19. For a trenchant account of land rights from a similarly broad vantage, see Lucy R. Lippard, *Undermining: A Wild Ride through Land Use, Politics, and Art in the Changing West* (New York: New Press, 2014).

20. See Kyle Whyte, "Settler Colonialism, Ecology, and Environmental Justice," *Environment and Society: Advances in Research* 9 (2018): 125–44; and Mishuana R. Goeman, "Disrupting a Settler-Colonial Grammar of Place: The Visual Memoir of Hulleah Tsinhnahjinnie," in *Theorizing Native Studies*, ed. Audra Simpson and Andrea Smith (Durham, NC: Duke University Press, 2014): 235–65.

Succession

1. Richard Serra, "Shift," in *Writings/Interviews* (Chicago: University of Chicago Press, 1994), 11.

2. Ibid., 12.

3. The property is currently managed by Great Gulf, a real estate company; hired by Hickory Hill, Great Gulf is not, as has been erroneously stated in some reporting, a subsidiary of Hickory Hill. Kathleen Schofield, executive vice president of land development for Great Gulf, correspondence with the author, July 26, 2017.

4. James Adams, "Richard Serra's Installation Shift Set to Become a Site of 'Cultural Heritage Value,'" *Globe and Mail*, February 26, 2013, https://www.theglobeandmail. com/arts/art-and-architecture/richard-serras-installation -shift-set-to-become-a-site-of-cultural-heritage-value /article9076831/ (accessed April 11, 2020).

5. See Oak Ridges Moraine Conservation Act, 2001, S.O. 2001, c. 31, https://www.ontario.ca/laws/statute/01031 (accessed April 11, 2020); see also the act's land use designations, http://www.mah.gov.on.ca/Page1743.aspx (accessed April 11, 2020).

6. On the food chain model, see Charles Elton, *Animal Ecology* (New York: Macmillan, 1927). The first cited use of the term "ecosystem" appears in A. G. Transley, "The Use and Abuse of Vegetational Concepts and Terms," *Ecology* 16, no. 3 (July 1935): 284–307.

7. For an influential summation of the steady-state model of ecology at the height of its influence, see Eugene P. Odum, "The Strategy of Ecosystem Development," *Science* 164, no. 3877 (April 18, 1969): 262–70.

8. Frederic E. Clements, *Plant Succession: An Analysis of the Development of Vegetation* (Washington, DC: Carnegie Institute, 1916).

9. The foundational text for this revision of succession is William H. Drury and Ian C. T. Nisbet, "Succession," *Journal of the Arnold Arboretum* 54, no. 3 (July 1973): 331–68.

10. Donald Worster, "The Ecology of Order and Chaos," *Environmental History Review* 14, nos. 1/2 (Spring/Summer 1990): 9.

11. See Clara Weyergraf-Serra and Martha Buskirk, eds., *The Destruction of Tilted Arc: Documents* (Cambridge, MA: MIT Press, 1991).

12. Richard Serra, "Pulitzer Arts Foundation Lecture," lecture delivered at Fogg Art Museum, Harvard University, April 16, 1988.

13. Ibid.

14. Richard Serra, quoted in Peter Goddard, "Rumours Swirl around Future of Richard Serra's Creation Shift," *Toronto Star*, January 27, 2008, https://www.thestar.com /opinion/columnists/2008/01/27/rumours_swirl _around_future_of_richard_serras_creation_shift.html (accessed July 24, 2020).

15. Since opening to the public in 1978, *Time Landscape* has subsequently been absorbed into New York's Greenstreets program, whose purpose is "to convert paved street properties, like triangles and malls, into green lawns." See New York City Department of Parks and Recreation, "Greenstreet: Time Landscape," https://

www.nycgovparks.org/parks/greenstreet-mz31/history
(accessed April 12, 2020).

16. Alan Sonfist, "Natural Phenomena as Public Monuments, 1968," in *Alan Sonfist: Natural History* (exhibition
catalog), ed. Alan Sonfist, Robert Slifkin, Stephanie
Snyder, and Allison Tepper (Portland, OR: Douglas F.
Cooley Memorial Art Gallery and Companion Editions,
2016), 14–15.

17. Alan Sonfist, conversation with the author, October 15,
2020.

18. Adrian Benepe, commissioner of the New York City
Department of Parks and Recreation, letter dated October
30, 2003, reprinted in Alan Sonfist, *Nature: The End of
Art: Environmental Landscapes* (Florence: Gli Ori, 2004),
243.

19. In a recent essay, Robert Slifkin similarly addresses
Time Landscape's dramatization of "the fundamental
relationship between natural and cultural forces," but
he arrives at a different conclusion regarding the work's
relationship to ruination. "*Time Landscape*," he writes,
"can be seen to be emblematic (if not prototypical) of the
ruin in the age of the Anthropocene, the period defined
by humanity's decisive impact on the Earth's ecosystem.
Sonfist's innovative conception of natural phenomena as
public monument—as well as his judicious acceptance
of the human mutations to his *Time Landscape*—present
a prescient vision of a world at once increasingly dominated by humankind and yet evermore bound to natural
systems beyond its control." "Alan Sonfist, Natural
History," in Sonfist et al., *Alan Sonfist: Natural History*, 22,
44–45.

20. Wilhelmine Hellmann, conversation with the author, June 18, 2019.

21. Nancy Kenney, "Nancy Holt's Desert Sun Tunnels Will Be Cleaned and Repaired—but the Bullet Marks Are Staying," *Art Newspaper*, April 25, 2019, https://www.theartnewspaper.com/news/holt-s-desert-sun-tunnels-will-be-cleaned-and-repaired-but-the-bullet-marks-are-staying (accessed April 12, 2020).

22. Richard McCoy, "Extending the Conservation Framework: A Site-Specific Conservation Discussion with Francesca Esmay," *art21* (July 21, 2009), http://magazine.art21.org/2009/07/21/extending-the-conservation-framework-a-site-specific-conservation-discussion-with-francesca-esmay/#.WZ9ouXeGORs (accessed April 12, 2020).

23. See Kirk Johnson, "Plans to Mix Oil Drilling and Art Clash in Utah," *New York Times*, March 27, 2008, https://www.nytimes.com/2008/03/27/us/27spiral.html (accessed April 12, 2020); Anny Shaw, "'No Intervention' Needed to Protect Spiral Jetty from Drought," *Art Newspaper*, September 25, 2015, https://www.theartnewspaper.com/news/no-intervention-needed-to-protect-spiral-jetty-from-drought (accessed April 12, 2020).

24. See Jeffrey Kastner, "Entropy and the New Monument," *Artforum* 46, no. 8 (April 2006): 167–70.

25. Carol Vogel, "Campaign Aims to Restore Weather-Abused 'Lightning Field,'" *New York Times*, June 7, 2012, https://www.nytimes.com/2012/06/08/arts/design/lightning-field-restoration-campaign-is-set.html (accessed April 12, 2020).

26. Smithson's commitment to entropy is raised in a
number of media reports that support Dia's decision not
to physically conserve the sculptural coil of *Spiral Jetty*.
See, for instance, Ben Eastham, "We Can't 'Save' Smithson's Spiral Jetty, and It Would Be Wrong to Try," *Apollo*
(October 8, 2015), https://www.apollo-magazine.com
/we-cant-save-smithsons-spiral-jetty-and-it-would-be
-wrong-to-try/ (accessed April 12, 2020). For an incisive
reading of entropy in Smithson's practice, see Caroline
A. Jones, "Entropies," in *Energies in the Arts*, ed. Douglas
Kahn (Cambridge, MA: MIT Press, 2019), 263–307.

27. Robert Smithson, "Cultural Confinement," in *Robert
Smithson: The Collected Writings*, ed. Jack Flam (Berkeley:
University of California Press, 1996), 155.

28. See Bob Colacello, "Remains of the Dia," *Vanity Fair*
(September 1996), https://www.vanityfair.com/maga-
zine/1996/09/colacello199609 (accessed July 24, 2020).
Letters archived in the Giuseppe Panza Papers at the
Getty Research Institute in Los Angeles also detail years
of updates and exchanges between founding members of
Dia and Panza, who was a significant early patron.

29. De Maria's initial sketch of *The Lightning Field* is held
in the Deiro Collection, Center for Art and Environment,
Nevada Museum of Art, box 33. On Dia and De Maria's
promotional strategies for the work, see Kenneth Baker,
The Lightning Field (New Haven, CT: Yale University Press,
2008); and James Nisbet, "A Brief Moment in the History
of Photo-Energy: Walter De Maria's *Lightning Field*," *Grey
Room* 50 (Winter 2013): 66–89.

30. Quoted in Hikmet Sidney Loe's indispensable recent
book, *The Spiral Jetty Encyclo: Exploring Robert Smithson's*

Earthwork through Time and Place (Salt Lake City: University of Utah Press, 2017), 70.

31. Robert Morris, "Anti Form," *Artforum* 6, no. 8 (April 1968): 33–35.

32. Nisbet, "The Art of Processing: Anti Form, Energy, and Ecological Materiality," in *Ecologies, Environments, and Energy Systems in Art of the 1960s and 1970s*, 129–79.

33. Umberto Eco, *The Open Work*, trans. Anna Cancogni (Cambridge, MA: Harvard University Press, 1989); Roland Barthes, "The Death of the Author," in *Image, Music, Text*, ed. and trans. Stephen Heath (New York: Farrar, Straus and Giroux, 1977), 142–48; Wolfgang Iser, *The Act of Reading: A Theory of Aesthetic Response* (Baltimore: Johns Hopkins University Press, 1978). Commissioned for and originally published in the issue of the experimental multimedia magazine *Aspen* dedicated to "Minimalism" (nos. 5/6, 1967), Barthes's text appeared alongside essays by George Kubler on "Style and the Representation of Historical Time" and Susan Sontag on "The Aesthetics of Silence."

Time Worlds

1. Robert Smithson, "The Spiral Jetty," in *Arts of the Environment*, ed. György Kepes (New York: Braziller, 1972), 229. As I discuss later, this essay not only describes the earthwork *Spiral Jetty* but is also a creative work of writing in its own right.

2. Robert Smithson, "Frederick Law Olmstead and the Dialectical Landscape," in Kepes, *Arts of the Environment*, 164.

3. See Steven R. Simms and Mark E. Stuart, "Ancient American Indian Life in the Great Salt Lake Wetlands: Archaeological and Biological Evidence," in *Great Salt Lake: An Overview of Change*, ed. J. Wallace Gwynn (Salt Lake City: Utah Geological Survey, 2002); and Hikmet Sidney Loe, "American Indians," in Loe, *The Spiral Jetty Encyclo*, 37–43.

4. The film *Mono Lake*, shot by Nancy Holt, Robert Smithson, and Michael Heizer in 1968, and edited by Holt in 2004, anticipates a number of the concerns that Smithson would soon address in his work at the Great Salt Lake. It is notable that a segment of the voiceover narration in *Mono Lake* acknowledges the Indigenous peoples of the Mono Basin region, but does so in a manner that places their presence in that region in the past, rather than continuing into the present day.

5. Heather Davis and Zoe Todd, "On the Importance of a Date, or Decolonizing the Anthropocene," *ACME: An International Journal for Critical Geographies* 16, no. 4 (2017): 772–73.

6. Ibid., 767. See also Kathryn Yusoff, *A Billion Black Anthropocenes or None* (Minneapolis: University of Minnesota Press, 2018); and T. J. Demos, *Against the Anthropocene: Visual Culture and the Environment Today* (New York: Sternberg, 2017).

7. See L. Anders Sandberg, Gerda R. Wekerle, and Liette Gilbert, *The Oak Ridges Moraine Battles: Development, Sprawl, and Nature Conservation in the Toronto Region* (Toronto: University of Toronto Press, 2013), 36.

8. Rebecca Belmore, *Facing the Monumental: Rebecca Belmore*, ed. Wanda Nanibush (Toronto and Fredericton, Canada: Art Gallery of Ontario and Goose Lane, 2018), 80.

9. Quoted by Candice Hopkins, curator of "Documenta 14," on Belmore's website, https://www.rebeccabelmore .com/biinjiyaiing-onji-from-inside/ (accessed April 12, 2020).

10. Mark Rifkin, *Beyond Settler Time: Temporal Sovereignty and Indigenous Self-Determination* (Durham, NC: Duke University Press, 2017), 3.

11. Johannes Fabian, *Time and the Other: How Anthropology Makes Its Object* (New York: Columbia University Press, 1983).

12. Marisol de la Cadena and Mario Blaser, eds., *A World of Many Worlds* (Durham, NC: Duke University Press, 2018). In their introduction, de la Cadena and Blaser describe the idea of "a world of many worlds" as a "pluriverse": "We propose the pluriverse as an analytic tool useful for producing ethnographic compositions capable of conceiving ecologies of practices across heterogenous(ly) entangled worlds" (4).

13. See, for instance, Ian L. McHarg, *Design with Nature* (Garden City, NY: American Museum of Natural History, 1969); Felicity D. Scott, *Architecture of Techno-Utopia: Politics after Modernism* (Cambridge, MA: MIT Press, 2007); and Anthony Vidler, "Whatever Happened to Ecology? John McHale and the Bucky Fuller Revival," *Log* 13/14 (Fall 2008): 139–46.

14. Kevin Lynch, *The Image of the City* (Cambridge, MA: MIT Press, 1960), 2. In the preface to this book, Lynch expressly notes the influence on his research of György Kepes, the Hungarian-born designer who taught at MIT from 1947 to 1974 and founded its Center for Advanced Visual Studies.

15. Kevin Lynch, *Site Planning* (Cambridge, MA: MIT Press, 1962), 1.

16. Ibid.

17. Kevin Lynch, *Wasting Away*, ed. Michael Southworth (San Francisco: Sierra Club Books, 1990).

18. Bonnie Devine, correspondence with the author, July 25, 2020.

19. Vanessa Watts, "Indigenous Place-Thought and Agency amongst Human and Non-humans (First Woman and Sky Woman Go on a European World Tour!)," *Decolonization: Indigeneity, Education, and Society* 2, no.1 (2013): 21.

20. Bonnie Devine, Tom Hill, Robert Houle, and Diane Pugen, *Stories from the Shield: Bonnie Devine* (Brantford, Canada: Woodland Cultural Centre, 2004), n.p., http://ccca.concordia.ca/c/writing/d/devine/dev002t.html (accessed April 12, 2020). On *Battle for the Woodlands*, see Ruth B. Phillips, "Between Rocks and Hard Places: Indigenous Lands, Settler Art Histories, and the 'Battle for the Woodlands,'" *Studies in Canadian Art, Architecture, and the Decorative Arts* 37, no. 1 (2016): 10–42; and Cheetham, *Landscape into Eco Art*, 84–87.

21. "Bonnie Devine: Anishinaabe (Ojibwe) and Member of Serpent River First Nation," https://resilienceproject.ca/en/artists/bonnie-devine (accessed July 24, 2020). A detail of the map painting from Devine's *Battle for the Woodlands* was included in the *Resilience Billboard Project* of 2018, which installed fifty billboards of artwork by Indigenous women across Canada.

22. "Bonnie Devine's Woodlands," video interview with Art Gallery of Ontario, posted December 11, 2015, https://www.youtube.com/watch?v=dbNbRho4fuQ (accessed July 24, 2020).

23. Ann O'Hanlon, "At a Rosslyn Park, Shadow Play," *Washington Post*, August 10, 2000, https://www.washingtonpost.com/archive/local/2000/08/10/at-a-rosslyn-park-shadow-play/2370b9f8-a842-4b1e-a008-c8ba5fc46a4c/ (accessed April 12, 2020).

24. Grateful Dead, "Dark Star," side A on *Dark Star/Born Crosseyed*, vinyl 7" (Warner Bros. Records, 1968).

25. herman de vries, "Chance and Change," in John K. Grande, *Art Nature Dialogues: Interviews with Environmental Artists* (Albany: State University of New York Press, 2004), 232.

26. Susanne Müller-Baji, "Kahlschlag im 'Heiligtum' auf der Prag," *Stuttgarter Zeitung*, March 25, 2018, https://www.stuttgarter-zeitung.de/inhalt.kunst-frevel-am-pragsattel-kahlschlag-im-heiligtum-auf-der-prag.a7bb5058-fc23-46ef-96c9-db710e77b14d.html (accessed July 24, 2020).

27. Jan Sellner, "Künstler will Klarstellung von der Stadt," *Stuttgarter Zeitung*, August 6, 2018, https://

www.stuttgarter-zeitung.de/inhalt.streit-um-kuns
twerk-in-stuttgart-kuenstler-will-klarstellung-von-der
-stadt.6641b38e-992a-41fc-bde6-2fecfc4b8c52.html
(accessed July 24, 2020). In a follow-up article, Sellner
notes that *Sanctuarium* presently does not qualify for
heritage status as a German monument because works
typically need to exist for at least a generation before
qualifying for consideration; see "Kunst wird nicht mehr
kleingehäckselt," *Stuttgarter Zeitung*, September 19, 2018,
https://www.stuttgarter-zeitung.de/inhalt.sanctuarium-
in-stuttgart-kunst-wird-nicht-mehr-kleingehaeckselt.
f88d751d-fea5-4a2b-ab5f-7ac1051d1e06.html (accessed
July 24, 2020).

28. On *Cadillac Ranch*, see Felicity D. Scott, *Living
Archive 7: Ant Farm, Allegorical Time Warp: The Media
Fallout of July 21, 1969* (New York: ACTAR, 2008); Con-
stance M. Lewallen and Steve Seid, *Ant Farm, 1968–1978*
(Berkeley: University of California Press, 2004); and Ant
Farm (written by Chip Lord), *Automerica: A Trip down
US Highways from World War II to the Future* (New York:
Dutton, 1976).

29. As Chip Lord explains: "*Cadillac Ranch* begins with
the 1949 tailfin and ends with 1964. Ten cars represent
each model change, not each consecutive year. For example, 1950, 1951, 1952, and 1953 are so similar, I almost
can't tell them apart. Then it's a big change in 1954, so
we have a 1954. 1955 and 1956 are very close, so we used
a 1956. But then 1957, 1958, 1959, and 1960 are each
so radical. The Detroit design idea was that if you can
change the model every year, why change it every three
years? Planned obsolescence." "Interview with Ant Farm:
Constance M. Lewallen in Conversation with Chip Lord,

Doug Michels, and Curtis Schreier," in Lewallen and Seid, *Ant Farm: 1968–1978*, 67.

30. Chip Lord, conversation with the author, June 27, 2019.

31. Stanley Marsh 3, who commissioned and owned the physical *Cadillac Ranch* sculpture (while Ant Farm retained its image rights), instigated the move of Ant Farm's work and owned the ABC affiliate that broadcast its twenty-year anniversary celebration. Marsh's children inherited the work following his death in 2014 and are currently in dialogue with the remaining members of Ant Farm regarding the long-term maintenance and potential restoration of *Cadillac Ranch*. Chip Lord, conversation with the author, June 27, 2019.

32. I recall first seeing *Cadillac Ranch* as a neon-colored painting on the wall of a Tony Roma's chain steakhouse in the 1990s. Ant Farm member Chip Lord has confirmed that Ant Farm did not provide licensing or receive payment for this and for many other popular uses of *Cadillac Ranch*. Ibid.

33. Ant Farm, *Cadillac Ranch* video, 1974/1994.

34. Chip Lord and Doug Michels, "Interview with Ant Farm," in Lewallen and Seid, *Ant Farm: 1968–1978*, 71.

35. See Chip Lord papers on Ant Farm, 1965–2014, Avery Drawings and Archives Collections, Columbia University, box 2.

36. Nancy Holt and Liza Béar, "Robert Smithson's *Amarillo Ramp*," *Avalanche* 8 (Fall 1973): 20.

37. Belmore has incorporated large megaphones into two outdoor sound installations. The first, *Ayum-ee-aawach Oomama-mowan: Speaking to Their Mother* (1991–1996, 2008), combines an electronic megaphone with a 6' × 7' cone made of wood and animal skin that amplifies its sound. *Ayum-ee-aawach Oomama-mowan* was first created in response to the 1990 "Oka Crisis," the land dispute standoff between Mohawk protesters and local and federal Canadian armed forces. It has subsequently been installed across numerous locations in North America to, in the artist's words, "address the land directly [as] an attempt to hear political protest as poetic action." Since 2007, *Ayum-ee-aawach Oomama-mowan* has been permanently installed at the Banff Centre for Arts and Creativity (https://www.rebeccabelmore.com/exhibit/Speaking-to-Their-Mother.html, accessed July 24, 2020). Belmore's second megaphone installation, *Wave Sound*, consists of four large, cast-aluminum cones that were placed as natural listening devices in different Canadian national parks as part of the exhibition "LandMarks2017 / Repères2017," staged for Canada's 150-year anniversary.

38. Edgar Heap of Birds, *Sharp Rocks* (Buffalo: CEPA, 1986), n.p. See also Bill Anthes, *Edgar Heap of Birds* (Durham, NC: Duke University Press, 2015).

Site-Images

1. Robert Smithson, "Art through the Camera's Eye," in Flam, ed., *Robert Smithson: The Collected Writings*, 372.

2. On land art's media networks, see, for instance, Pamela M. Lee, "Ultramoderne: Or, How George Kubler

Stole the Time in Sixties Art," in *Chronophobia: On Time in the Art of the 1960s* (Cambridge, MA: MIT Press, 2004), 218–56; Andrew V. Uroskie, "Le Jetée en Spirale: Robert Smithson's Stratigraphic Cinema," *Grey Room* 19 (Spring 2005): 54–79; Felicity D. Scott, "Shouting Apocalypse," in *Architecture or Techno-Utopia: Politics after Modernism* (Cambridge, MA: MIT Press, 2007), 210–45; Jane McFadden, "Earthquakes, Photoworks, and Oz: Walter de Maria's Conceptual Art," *Art Journal* 68, no. 3 (Fall 2009): 68–87; and Philipp Kaiser and Miwon Kwon, "Ends of the Earth and Back," in *Ends of the Earth: Land Art to 1974* (exhibition catalog), ed. Philipp Kaiser and Miwon Kwon (Los Angeles: Museum of Contemporary Art, 2012), 17–31.

3. On *Spiral Jetty*'s media, see Eugenie Tsai and Cornelia Butler, *Robert Smithson* (exhibition catalog) (Berkeley: University of California Press, 2004); Lynne Cooke and Karen Kelly, eds., *Robert Smithson: Spiral Jetty, True Fictions, False Realities* (Berkeley: University of California Press, 2005); and Loe, *The Spiral Jetty Encyclo.*

4. For published examples of Gorgoni's photographs of *Shift*, see Richard Serra and Clara Weyergraf, *Richard Serra: Interviews, Etc. 1970–1980* (exhibition catalog) (New York: Hudson River Museum, 1980); Rosalind E. Krauss, *Richard Serra/Sculpture* (exhibition catalog), ed. Laura Rosenstock (New York: Museum of Modern Art, 1986); Hal Foster and Gordon Hughes, eds., *Richard Serra (October Files)* (Cambridge, MA: MIT Press, 2000); Kynaston McShine, *Richard Serra Sculpture: Forty Years* (exhibition catalog) (New York: Museum of Modern Art, 2007); and Kaiser and Kwon, *Ends of the Earth: Land Art to 1974.*

5. Smithson, "The Spiral Jetty," 222–32. See Ann Wolfe, *Gianfranco Gorgoni: Land Art Photographs* (exhibition catalog) (New York: Monacelli, 2021). My thanks to Bill Fox and Sara Frantz for drawing my attention to this publication.

6. Gorgoni published many of these photographs in Grégoire Müller and Gianfranco Gorgoni, *The New Avant-Garde: Issues for the Art of the Seventies* (New York: Praeger, 1972); and Gianfranco Gorgoni, *Beyond the Canvas: Artists of the Seventies and Eighties* (New York: Rizzoli, 1985).

7. Gianfranco Gorgoni, correspondence with the author, March 15, 2018.

8. A representative selection of these techniques in contemporary photographic practice appears in Sarah Greenough, *The Memory of Time* (exhibition catalog) (Washington, DC: National Gallery of Art, 2015).

9. Annette Michelson, "Robert Morris: An Aesthetics of Transgression," in *Robert Morris* (exhibition catalog) (Washington, DC: Corcoran Gallery of Art, 1969); Rosalind Krauss, "Notes on the Index: Seventies Art in America," *October* 3 (Spring 1977): 68–81; and Rosalind Krauss, "Notes on the Index: Seventies Art in America, Part 2," *October* 4 (Fall 1977): 58–67.

10. Roland Barthes, *Camera Lucida: Reflections on Photography*, trans. Richard Howard (New York: Hill and Wang, 1980), 85.

11. Charles S. Peirce, "One, Two, Three: Fundamental Categories of Thought and of Nature," and "An Elementary Account of the Logic of Relatives," in *Writings of*

Charles S. Peirce: A Chronological Edition, vol. 5, *1884–1886* (Bloomington: Indiana University Press, 1993), 245, 379.

12. Nancy Holt, "Pine Barrens," *Avalanche* 11 (Summer 1975): 6.

13. Hayden Pedigo, *Greetings from Amarillo*, released digitally and on 12" vinyl (Driftless Recordings, 2017).

14. Félix Guattari, *The Three Ecologies*, trans. Ian Pindar and Paul Sutton (London: Athlone, 2000), 44.

Image Credits

Figure 1: Courtesy of Go Lake Havasu

Figure 2: © 2021 Holt/Smithson Foundation and Dia Art Foundation, licensed by VAGA at Artists Rights Society (ARS), NY

Figure 3: © 2021 Holt/Smithson Foundation and Dia Art Foundation, licensed by VAGA at Artists Rights Society (ARS), NY

Figure 4: © Estate of Hollis Frampton

Figure 5: © 2021 Holt/Smithson Foundation, licensed by VAGA at Artists Rights Society (ARS), NY

Figure 6: © 2021 Holt/Smithson Foundation, licensed by VAGA at Artists Rights Society (ARS), NY

Figure 7: © Agnes Denes, courtesy Leslie Tonkonow Artworks + Projects, New York

Figure 8: © Agnes Denes, courtesy Leslie Tonkonow Artworks + Projects, New York

Figure 9: Photograph © San Francisco Chronicle/Polaris, artwork by kind permission of the artist and FOR-SITE Foundation

Figure 10: By kind permission of Richard Serra

Figure 11: By kind permission of Richard Serra

Figure 12: By kind permission of the photographer

Figure 13: By the author

Figure 14: By kind permission of Richard Serra

Figure 15: By kind permission of Alan Sonfist

Figure 16: By kind permission of Alan Sonfist

Figure 17: © 2021 Holt/Smithson Foundation and Dia Art Foundation, licensed by VAGA at Artists Rights Society (ARS), NY

Figure 18: By kind permission of Rebecca Belmore

Figure 19: By kind permission of Bonnie Devine

Figure 20: By kind permission of Bonnie Devine and Art Gallery of Ontario

Figure 21: © 2021 Holt/Smithson Foundation, licensed by VAGA at Artists Rights Society (ARS), NY

Figure 22: By kind permission of herman de vries

Figure 23: By kind permission of Chip Lord

Figure 24: By kind permission of Chip Lord

Figure 25: By kind permission of Chip Lord

Figure 26: © 2021 Holt/Smithson Foundation, licensed by VAGA at Artists Rights Society (ARS), NY

Figure 27: By kind permission of Rebecca Belmore and Walter Phillips Gallery, Banff Centre for Arts and Creativity

Figure 28: By kind permission of Edgar Heap of Birds

Figure 29: Image provided by Getty Research Institute, Los Angeles (2008.R.6), artwork © Michael Heizer/Triple Aught Foundation, photograph © Maya Gorgoni

Figure 30: Photograph © Maya Gorgoni; artwork by kind permission of Richard Serra

Figure 31: Photograph © Maya Gorgoni; artwork © 2021 Holt/Smithson Foundation and Dia Art Foundation, licensed by VAGA at Artists Rights Society (ARS), NY

Figure 32: © 2021 Holt/Smithson Foundation, licensed by VAGA at Artists Rights Society (ARS), NY

Figure 33: © 2021 Holt/Smithson Foundation, licensed by VAGA at Artists Rights Society (ARS), NY

Figure 34: By kind permission of Chip Lord